The Little Book

of

GREAT

PUT-DOWNS

The Little Book
of
GREAT
PUT-DOWNS

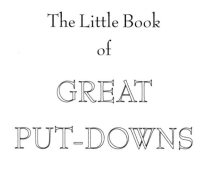

Edited by

ROSANNA KELLY

Parragon
Queen Street House
4 Queen Street
Bath BA1 1HE

Special Edition for PAST TIMES®, Oxford, England, 1999

Produced by Magpie Books, an imprint of
Robinson Publishing Ltd, London

ISBN 0 75252 684 7

A copy of the British Library Cataloguing-in-Publication Data
is available from the British Library

Printed in China

PAST TIMES®

Contents

Introduction

Most of us think of the insults we wish we had said when it is too late. Here is a book that not only contains insults to suit every occasion, but is small enough to be ready to hand in your pocket. As Churchill once said of himself: "It is a good thing for an uneducated man to read books of quotations."

The Shorter Oxford Dictionary gives two definitions of the word insult. The first is "an open and sudden attack without formal preparation, an action causing injury to the body or disturbance of its normal functions"; the second is "to treat with scornful abuse." In this book we find examples of both types, from Walter Raleigh boxing his son's ear to Oscar Wilde's comment on Bernard Shaw: "He hasn't an enemy in the world, and none of his friends like him."

We start with insults for Social Occasions. When forced into the company of someone you dislike, would you, like Groucho Marx, insult them by saying "I've had a wonderful evening. But this wasn't it"? Discontented travelers will find their prejudices confirmed in People and Places. The Arts, *beginning with literature and painting and concluding with the performing arts, contains much damning criticism, and there are fierce exchanges in* The War of the Sexes. *Lord Chesterfield maintained that "the only lasting peace between a man and his wife is, doubtless, a separation": there is much evidence to support this. In* Politics *the insult is almost an art form;* Parting Shots *is a collection of summings-up and puttings-down.*

I should like to thank Adrian and Marina Berry, Eleanor Berry, Caroline Brooke-Johnson, Anthony Grigg, Casilda Grigg, Rachel Grigg, Michael Hartwell, Laurence Kelly, Katherine Kjellgren, Thomas Pakenham, Guy Philipps, Sergei Reviakin, Maria Winner, Jan and Yura Usvyat, and Theo Vassilieff for their help in providing insults for the book without offending me in the process, and thanks above all to my mother, Linda Kelly.

Chapter 1

SOCIAL OCCASIONS

The English biographer Lytton Strachey wasted no words in conversation. A young and robust friend of ours, Constant Lambert, meeting him at a party, said: "You don't remember, Mr Strachey? We met four years ago." "Quite a nice interval, I think, don't you?" remarked Mr Strachey pleasantly, and passed on.

Edith Sitwell, *Taken Care Of*

On social occasions the best insults are often – though not always – concealed by a veneer of good manners.

I've had a perfectly wonderful evening. But this wasn't it.

Groucho Marx

The General told us, that when he was a very young man, I think only fifteen, serving under Prince Eugene of Savoy, he was sitting in a company at table with a Prince of Wirtemberg. The Prince took up a glass of wine, and, by a fillip, made some of it fly in Oglethorpe's face. Here was a nice dilemma. To have challenged him instantly, might have fixed a quarrelsome character upon the young soldier: to have taken no notice of it, might have been considered as cowardice. Oglethorpe, therefore, keeping his eye upon the Prince and smiling all the time, as if he took what his Highness had done in jest, said: "Mon Prince" – (I forget the French words he used, the purport however was) "That's a good joke; but we do it much better in England"; And threw a whole glass of wine in the Prince's face. An old general, who sat by, said, "Il a bien fait, mon prince, vous l'avez commencé": and thus all ended in good humour.

Dinner at General Oglethorpe's, 10 April 1772:
Boswell, Life of Johnson

Lord Glasgow, having flung a waiter through the window of his club, brusquely ordered: "Put him on the bill."

Guy Phillips, *Bad Behaviour*

Dinner at the Huntercombes possessed only two dramatic features – the wine was a farce and the food was a tragedy.

Anthony Powell, *The Acceptance World*

Would-be conversationalist: Do you know the story about the Englishman, the Irishman and the Scotsman?
Greta Garbo: I wish they'd never met.

Attrib.

Oscar Wilde: How I wish I'd said that.
Whistler: You will, Oscar, you will.

Richard Ellmann, *Oscar Wilde*

I think this wine has been drunk before.

Anon

… vice leaning on the arm of crime, Monsieur de Talleyrand supported by Monsieur Fouché …

Chateaubriand's description of Talleyrand and Fouché at an audience with King Louis XVIII: René de Chateaubriand, *Mémoires*

There goes the famous good time that was had by all.

Bette Davis

I was profoundly grateful to Mr Jowett, but being constantly asked to breakfast alone with him was a terrible ordeal. Sometimes he never spoke at all, and would only walk round the room looking at me with unperceiving, absent eyes as I ate my bread and butter, in a way that, for a very nervous boy, was utterly terrific. Walking with this kind and silent friend was even worse: he scarcely ever spoke, and if, in my shyness, I said something at one milestone, he would make no response at all until we reached the next, when he would say abruptly, "Your last observation was singularly commonplace," and relapse into silence again.

Of Benjamin Jowett, Master of Balliol College,
Oxford: Augustus Hare, *The Story of My Life*

❧

The "t" is silent, as in Harlow.
Margot Asquith to the film star Jean Harlow
who had been mispronouncing her first name:
T.S. Mathews, *Great Tom*

On their last night at Calcutta, General Grant and "Suite" – with the exception of Mrs. Grant (who was "incommoded in her inside") dined with the Chief Justice Sir R. Garth and Lady Garth, from whose house they embarked. On this occasion "our distinguished guest" the double Ex-President of the "Great Western Republic," who got as drunk as a fiddle, showed that he could also be as profligate as a lord. He fumbled Mrs. A., kissed the shrieking Miss B. – pinched the plump Mrs C. black and blue – and ran at Miss D. with intent to ravish her.

Finally, after throwing all the Garths' female guests into hysterics by generally behaving like a must elephant, the noble beast was captured by main force and carried (*quatre pattes dans l'air*) by six sailors on board the ship which relieved India of his distinguished presence.

A visit to Calcutta in 1880 of the former President
of the United States, Ulysses S. Grant:
Robert, Lord Lytton, Viceroy of India,
in a letter to a friend

A petty, sneaking rogue I knew –
O! Mr Cr – , how do ye do?

> William Blake (of a Mr Cromek),
> *On Friends and Foes*

⁓❦⁓

Gentleman on the street: Mr Jones, I believe?
Duke of Wellington: If you believe that, you'll believe
anything.

> Elizabeth Longford, *Pillar of State*

⁓❦⁓

The Dr (Ralph Kettel) tastes the wine: – "What," said
he, "didst thou take this drink out of a ditch?" and
when he saw the cheese-cakes:- "What have we here,
crinkum crankum?"

> John Aubrey, *Brief Lives*

Very sorry can't come. Lie follows by post.
> Telegram from Lord Charles Beresford to the
> Prince of Wales, later Edward VII, when he was
> summoned to dine at the eleventh hour:
> R. Nevill, *The World of Fashion 1837–1922*

Good God, do you mean to say this place is a club!
> F.E. Smith on being reproved by the secretary of
> the Atheneaum, of which he was not a member,
> for using it as a convenience on his way to the
> House of Lords: attrib.

CECILY: Do you suggest, Miss Fairfax, that I entrapped Ernest into an engagement? How dare you? This is no time for wearing the shallow mask of manners. When I see a spade I call it a spade.

GWENDOLEN (*Satirically*): I am glad to say that I have never seen a spade. It is obvious that our social spheres have been widely different.

Enter MERRIMAN *followed by the* FOOTMAN. *He carries a salver, table cloth and plate stand.* CECILY *is about to retort. The presence of the servants exercises a restraining influence, under which both girls chafe.*

MERRIMAN: Shall I lay tea here as usual, miss?

CECILY: (*Sternly, in a calm voice*): Yes, as usual.

MERRIMAN *begins to clear table and lay cloth. A long pause.* CECILY *and* GWENDOLEN *glare at each other.*

GWENDOLEN: Are there many interesting walks in the vicinity, Miss Cardew?

CECILY: Oh! Yes! a great many. From the top of one of the hills quite close one can see five counties.

GWENDOLEN: Five counties! I don't think I should like that. I hate crowds.

CECILY: (*Sweetly*) I suppose that is why you live in a town?

GWENDOLEN *bites her lip, and beats her foot nervously with her parasol.*

GWENDOLEN (*Looking round*): Quite a well-kept garden this is, Miss Cardew.

CECILY: So glad you like it, Miss Fairfax.

GWENDOLEN: I had no idea there were any flowers in the country.

CECILY: Oh, flowers are as common here, Miss Fairfax, as people are in London … May I offer you some tea, Miss Fairfax?

GWENDOLEN: (With elaborate politeness): Thank you. (*Aside*) Detestable girl! But I require tea!

CECILY (*Sweetly*): Sugar?

GWENDOLEN (*Superciliously*) No, thank you. Sugar is not fashionable any more.

CECILY *looks angrily at her, takes up the tongs, and puts four lumps of sugar into the cup.*

CECILY (*Severely*): Cake or bread and butter?

GWENDOLEN (*In a bored manner*): Bread and butter, please. Cake is rarely seen at the best houses nowadays.

CECILY (*Cuts a very large slice of cake, and puts it on the tray.*) Hand that to Miss Fairfax.

MERRIMAN *does so, and goes out with the* FOOTMAN

GWENDOLEN *drinks the tea and makes a grimace. Puts down cup at once, reaches out her hand to the bread and butter, looks at it and finds it is cake. Rises in indignation.*

GWENDOLEN: You have filled my tea with lumps of sugar, and though I asked you most distinctly for bread and butter, you have given me cake. I am known for the gentleness of my disposition, and the extraordinary sweetness of my nature, but I warn you, Miss Cardew, you may go too far.

Oscar Wilde, *The Importance of Being Earnest*

~ ❀ ~

Talleyrand, on being button-holed by a bore in the Traveller's Club, called over one of the servants and said: "Do you mind listening to the end of this man's story."

John Train, *Wit*

~ ❀ ~

Now there sits a man with an open mind. You can feel the draught from here.

Groucho Marx

Sir Walter, being strangely surprised and put out of his countenance at so great a table, gives his son a damned blow over the face. His son, as rude as he was, would not strike his father, but strikes over the face the gentleman that sat next to him and said: "Box about: 'twill come to my father anon."

John Aubrey, *Brief Lives*

A lady sitting next to F.E. Smith at a dinner party explained that she "could never eat tongue because it came from an animal's mouth."

"Try an egg," said Smith.

Attrib.

More of your conversation would infect my brain.

William Shakespeare, *Coriolanus*

At a dinner party, the story went, she (Princess Anne) talked to one of her neighbours about horses throughout the whole meal, utterly ignoring the other. At last she turned: "Could I have the sugar please?" The slighted young man placed two lumps on his palm and held them out to the hippomane.

Elizabeth Longford,
The Oxford Book of Royal Anecdotes

~•~

"I shall be sure to say three dull things as soon as ever I open my mouth, shan't I – (looking round with the most good humoured dependence on everybody's assent): – 'Do not you all think I shall?'"
Emma could not resist.
"Ah! ma'am, but there may be a difficulty. Pardon me but you will be limited as to number – only three at once."

Miss Bates and Emma Woodhouse at a picnic on Box Hill: Jane Austen, *Sense and Sensibility*

Lord Thanet had invited several of his country neighbours to dine with him and had entreated of Lady Thanet that she would treat them with civility, which she promised to do. When they were assembled, she came into the drawing room and after the common bows and curtsies, she said, "Gentlemen, I beg you will be on no ceremony here – do exactly as if you were at home – get upon all fours."

Lord Glenhervie's diary, 29 October 1796

Certainly there is nothing else here to enjoy.
Bernard Shaw when his hostess at a party asked him if he was enjoying himself: attrib.

LADY SNEER (*of Miss Vermilion*): Oh, surely she is a pretty woman.

CRABTREE: I am very glad you think so, ma'am.

MRS CANDOUR: She has a charming fresh colour.

LADY TEAZLE: Yes, when it is fresh put on.

MRS CANDOUR: Oh, fie! I'll swear I have seen it come and go!

LADY TEAZLE: I dare swear you have, ma'am: it goes off at night, and comes again in the morning.

> Lady Teazle's drawing room:
> Richard Brinsley Sheridan, *The School for Scandal*

C'était donc, Monsieur votre père qui n'était pas beau. (So, it was Monsieur your father who was the bad-looking one.)

> Talleyrand, bored by a young man who was boasting of his mother's beauty: John Train, *Wit*

Look here, Steward, if this is coffee, I want tea; but if this is tea then I wish for coffee.

Punch, 1902

Do you suppose I could buy back my introduction to you?

Groucho Marx in the film *Monkey Business*

Good night all. So lovely to have been among friends, even if they weren't mine.

Anon

Yes, I agree, he [Macaulay] is certainly more agreeable since his return from India. His enemies might perhaps have said before (though I never did so) that he talked rather too much; but now he has occasional flashes of silence that make his conversation perfectly delightful.

> Sydney Smith of Thomas Babington Macaulay:
> Trevelyan, *Macaulay*

You know the kind of thing – the salad was decorated with the Lord's Prayer in beetroot.

> Margot Asquith of Lady Desborough's
> excessively elaborate food: attrib.

His idea of fun is throwing an egg in an electric fan.

> Anon

"I rather like bad wine," said Mr Mountchesney, "one gets so bored with good wine."

> Disraeli, *Sybil*

"Oh, I must try some, if it is an Indian dish," said Miss Rebecca. "I am sure everything must be good that comes from there."

"Give Miss Sharp some curry, my dear," said Mr Sedley, laughing.

Rebecca had never tasted the dish before.

"Do you find it as good as everything else from India?" said Mr Sedley, laughing.

"Oh, excellent!" said Rebecca, who was suffering tortures with the cayenne pepper.

"Try a chili with it, Miss Sharp," said Joseph, really interested.

"A chili," said Rebecca, gasping. "O yes!" She thought a chili was something cool, as its name imported and was served with some. "How fresh and green they look!" she said, and put one into her mouth. It was hotter than the curry; flesh and blood could bear it no longer. She laid down her fork. "Water, for Heaven's sake, water!" she cried. Mr Sedley burst out laughing (he was a coarse man, from the Stock Exchange, where they love all sorts of practical jokes). They are real Indian, I assure you," said he.

William Makepeace Thackeray, *Vanity Fair*

[Whitman] was not only eager to talk about himself but reluctant to have the conversation stray from the subject for too long.

Henry Thoreau on Walt Whitman: Paul Johnson,
A History of the American People

She talks like a revolving door.

Anon

Dear Frank, we believe you; you have dined in every house in London – *once.*
Oscar Wilde interrupting Frank Harris's long-winded account of the houses he had dined at: attrib.

He [the Shah of Persia, Nasr-ed-Din] knows no English and very few words of French, but when the Baroness Coutts, as the great benefactress of her country, was presented to him by the Prince of Wales, he looked in her face and exclaimed, "Quelle horreur!"

The Shah of Persia on a visit to England in July 1889: A.J.C. Hare, *The Story of My Life*

He dances like a cattle stampede.

Anon

My good man, I'm not a strawberry.

Edward VII's rebuke to a footman who had spilt cream on him: C. Asiat, *The Last Country Houses*

MARIA: [Aside] Their malice is intolerable! [Aloud] Lady Sneerwell: I must wish you a good morning. I'm not very well. *Exit*

MRS CANDOUR: O dear, she chang'd colour very much –!

LADY SNEERWELL: Do Mrs Candour follow her – she may want assistance.

MRS CANDOUR: That I will with all my soul. Ma'am – poor dear Girl – who knows – what her situation may be.

Richard Brinsley Sheridan, *School for Scandal*

This piece of cod passes all understanding.

At a restaurant, Sir Edwin Lutyens: attrib.

We've all heard soup gargled and siphoned, but he yodels it.

Anon

Madam, before you flatter a man so grossly to his face, you should consider whether or not your flattery is worth having.

Dr Johnson: in *Fanny Burney, Diary and Letters*

His wife always begs him: "Now if it's a dull party, just leave it that way."

Anon

A pompous woman of his acquaintance, complaining that the head-waiter of a restaurant had not shown her and her husband immediately to a table, said, "We had to tell him who we were." Gerald, interested, enquired, "And who were you?"

Edith Sitwell, *Taken Care Of*

As soon as that man's tongue stops, that woman's begins!

Samuel Rogers of Jane and Thomas Carlyle
at a breakfast party: Francis Espinasse,
Literary Recollections and Sketches

One very hot evening in summer, Lady Holland and a large party of friends were suffering from the stifling atmosphere, and a general dulness had crept over the company. Then [Monckton] Milnes was seen to enter. "Ah here comes the cool of the evening," cried Sydney Smith and immediately everyone grew brighter. [Milnes resented this and other nicknames, and Smith wrote to him: "The names of 'Cool of the Evening,' 'London Assurance,' and 'In-I-go-Jones,' are, I give you my word, not mine."]

T. Wemyss Reid, *Life of Lord Houghton*

"Cad," said Sir Grummore.

"Yah," said King Pellinore.

They turned round and marched off to their corners, seething with indignation.

"Swindler," shouted Sir Grummore.

"Beastly bully," shouted King Pellinore.

With this they summoned all their energies together for one decisive encounter, leaned forward, lowered their heads like two billy-goats, and positively sprinted together for the final blow.

The joust between Sir Grummore and King Pellinore:
T.H. White, *The Once and Future King*

... I am sure
Though you know what temperance should be,
You know not what it is.

William Shakespeare, *Anthony and Cleopatra*

He [W.H. Auden] always got on well with Mrs Carritt, even though at breakfast on the first morning he tasted his tea and then said flatly, "Mrs Carritt, this tea is like tepid piss."

Charles Osborne, *W.H. Auden: The Life of a Poet*

~•~

As the rain poured down and his shoot seemed doomed he muttered: "How like God."

Sir William Eden, *Tribulations of a Baronet*

~•~

… turning round, he looked for a moment at Elizabeth, till catching her eye, he withdrew his own and coldly said, "She is tolerable, but not handsome enough to tempt me; and I am in no humour at present to give consequence to young ladies who are slighted by other men …"

Mr Darcy's insolence to Elizabeth Bennet at the dance: Jane Austen, *Pride and Prejudice*

When someone asked him how best to answer the American greeting, "Pleased to meet you," Lord Hartington replied, "I should say 'And so you damned well ought to be.'"

Jonathan Garnier Ruffen, *The Big Shots*

… Thy food is such
As hath been belch'd on by infected lungs.

Marina to the servant Boult:
William Shakespeare, *Pericles*

An acquaintance having, in a morning call bored him [Beau Brummell] dreadfully about some tour he had done in the north of England, enquired with great pertinacity of his impatient listener which of the lakes he preferred; when Brummell quite tired of the man's tedious raptures turned his head imploringly towards his valet ...

"Robinson."

"Sir."

"Which of the lakes do I admire?"

"Windermere, sir," replied that distinguished individual.

"Ah, yes – Windermere" – repeated Brummell, "so it is – Windermere."

Captain William Jesse, Beau Brummell: quoted in Ellen Moer's, *The Dandy*

In 1921 when Queen Mary received an honorary degree at Oxford, Lord Curzon, as Chancellor of the University arranged a luncheon for her at Balliol.

Only the unremitting attention he gave to the smallest detail of any such occasion saved it from what in his eyes might have been a social disaster. While preparing for the entertainment, the Bursar of Balliol sent the Chancellor a specimen menu. Curzon returned it with a single sentence written across one corner. "Gentlemen do not take soup at luncheon."

Kenneth Rose, *Superior Person*

Peas and beans are as dank here as a dog, and that is
The best way to give poor jades the bots.

William Shakespeare, *Henry IV, part I*

If Mr Selwyn calls again, shew him up; if I am alive I shall be delighted to see him; and if I am dead he would like to see me.

Henry Fox, first Baron Holland, last words:
J.H. Jesse, *George Selwyn and his Contemporaries*

Chapter 2

PEOPLE AND PLACES

Frogs ... are slightly better than Huns or Wops, but abroad is unutterably bloody and foreigners are fiends.

Uncle Matthew in Nancy Mitford,
The Pursuit of Love

Travel does not always broaden the mind, as Uncle Matthew's reactions make clear.

It is absurd to say that there are neither ruins nor curiosities in America when they have their mothers and their accents.

Oscar Wilde

~ 🌑 ~

In Italy for thirty years under the Borgias they had warfare, terror, murder, bloodshed – they produced Michelangelo, Leonardo da Vinci and the Renaissance. In Switzerland they had brotherly love, five hundred years of democracy and peace and what did that produce ... ? The cuckoo clock.

Orson Welles, words added to Graham Greene's film script, *The Third Man*

~ 🌑 ~

A soggy little island huffing and puffing to keep up with Western Europe.

Of England: John Updike, *Picked up Pieces*

There is never any doubt, then, that one has arrived in Spain ... There is a faint sound of drums, a smell of crude olive oil, and current of strong, leaking electricity.

Anthony Carson, *A Train to Andalusia*

Interviewer: Have you found any professional criticism of your work illuminating or helpful. Edmund Wilson, for example?
Evelyn Waugh: Is he an American?
Interviewer: Yes.
Waugh: I don't think what they have to say is of much interest, do you?

Evelyn Waugh, interviewed in *The Paris Review*

Norway, too, has noble wild prospects, and Lapland is remarkable for prodigious noble wild prospects. But, Sir, let me tell you, the noblest prospect which a Scotchman ever sees, is the high road that leads him to England!

Boswell, *Life of Johnson*

Taffy was a Welshman
Taffy was a thief
Taffy came to my house
And stole a piece of beef.

English nursery rhyme

England is a nation of shopkeepers.
Napoleon I: Barry E. O'Meara, *Napoleon in Exile*

To God I speak Spanish, to women Italian, to men French, and to my horse – German.

Charles V, Holy Roman Emperor: attrib.

To live in Australia permanently is rather like going to a party and dancing all night with one's mother.

Barry Humphries

I know why the sun never sets on the British Empire – God wouldn't trust an Englishman in the dark.

Duncan Spaeth: Nancy McPhee, *The Book of Insults*

I hate the French because they are all slaves and wear wooden shoes.

Oliver Goldsmith, *Essays*

Dried fish is a staple food in Iceland… it varies in toughness. The tougher kind tastes like toe-nails, and the softer kind like the skin off the soles of one's feet.

W.H. Auden and Louis MacNiece, *Letters from Iceland*

America is a country that doesn't know where it is going, but is determined to set a speed record getting there.

Peter Lawrence

In matters of commerce the fault of the Dutch
Is offering too little and asking too much.

George Canning, Dispatch, in cipher, to the English ambassador at the Hague

I don't want to live in a city where the only cultural advantage is you can make a right turn on a red light.

Woody Allen about Los Angeles in *Annie Hall* (film)

Only a Carpathian would come back to life now and choose New York.

Ghostbusters (film)

The Sussex men are noted fools,
And weak is their brain-pan;
I wonder if H – the painter
Is not a Sussex man?

William Blake (of the painter William Haines),
On Friends and Foes

The great virtues of the German people have created
more evil than idleness ever did vices.

Paul Valéry, *La Crise de l'Ésprit*

∽⟨♠⟩∼

America is one long expectoration.

Oscar Wilde

∽⟨♠⟩∼

Manchester with a harbour backdrop.

Robert Morley of Sydney, Australia

∽⟨♠⟩∼

France has neither winter nor summer nor morals –
apart from these drawbacks it is a fine country.

Mark Twain, *Notebooks*

I am willing to love all mankind, except an American.
Dr Johnson

The actor George Cooke was hissed in Liverpool and stopped acting to denounce the audience: "There is not one brick in this dirty town that has not been cemented with the blood of a negro slave."
Attrib.

That knuckle-end of England – that land of Calvin, oatcakes and sulphur.
Sydney Smith on Scotland: Lady Holland,
Memoir, 1855

It was wonderful to find America, but it would have been more wonderful to miss it.

Mark Twain

To speak of Iceland is little need;
Save of stockfish.

Haklyut: W.H. Auden and Louis MacNeice,
Letters from Iceland

What an Englishman cares to invent, a Frenchman to design, or a German to patch together, the stupid Pole will buy and the Russian will deprive him of it.

Polish saying

A servile race in folly nursed,
Who truckle most when treated worst.

> Of the Irish: Jonathan Swift

... a long despotism tempered by epigrams.

> Of France: Thomas Carlyle,
> *History of the French Revolution*

Continental people have sex-life; the English have hot-water bottles.

> George Mikes, *How to be an Alien*

Knavery seems to be so much the striking feature of its inhabitants that it may not in the end be an evil that they will become aliens to this country.

> Of America: George III

So you're going to Australia! ... What are you going to sing? All I can say is — sing 'em muck! It's all they can understand!

Dame Nellie Melba to Clara Butt

All these financiers, all the little gnomes in Zurich and the other financial centres about whom we keep on hearing.

Harold Wilson (Baron Wilson of Rievalulx),
Hansard, 12 November 1956

The English plays are like their English puddings: nobody has any taste for them but themselves.

Voltaire (François-Marie Arouet)

Vermont! You don't mean that narrow, pinched-up, little state on the wrong side of Boston?... What are you going to do there between yawns?

Bette Davis to George Brent in *Dark Victory* (film)

Ireland is the old sow that eats her farrow.

James Joyce, *Portrait of the Artist as a Young Man*

Serve the German with your heart;
Your reward will be a fart.

Polish saying

Curse the blasted, jelly-boned swines, the slimy, the belly-wriggling invertebrates, the miserable sodding rotters, the flaming sods, the nivelling, dribbling, palsied, pulseless lot that make up England. They've got white of egg in their veins, and their spunk is that watery it's a marvel they can breed. They can nothing but frogspawn the gibberers. Why, why, why, was I born an Englishman!

D.H. Lawrence, after the rejection of his manuscript,
Sons and Lovers

Australians are still too conservative for anatomically correct dolls.

Anonymous spokesman for the
Australian Toy Trade, 1969

Very flat, Norfolk.

Noel Coward, *Private Lives*

It's about the end of the world and God knows, this place is the absolute end.

> Ava Gardner to Australian pressmen about her film
> *On the Beach*

France is a dog-hole.

> William Shakespeare, *All's Well that Ends Well*

This gloomy region, where the year is divided into one day and one night, lies entirely outside the stream of history.

> Of Canada: W.W. Reade

Of all noxious animals, too, the most noxious is a tourist. And of all tourists the most vulgar, ill-bred, offensive and loathsome is the British tourist.

Rev. Francis Kilvert, *Diary*, 5 April 1876

Dublin, though a place much worse than London, is not so bad as Iceland.

Dr Johnson, Letter to Mrs Christopher Smart, 1791

I don't even know what street Canada is on.

Al Capone

A verb has a hard time enough of it in the world when it's all together. It's downright inhuman to split it up. But that's just what those Germans do. They take part of a verb and put it down here, like a stake, and then take the other part of it and put it away over yonder and between these two limits thay just shovel in German.

Mark Twain, Address at a dinner of the Nineteenth Century Club, New York, 1900

Italy is a geographical expression.

Prince Metternich, Letter, November 1849

Sir, they are a race of convicts and ought to be grateful for anything we allow them short of hanging.

Of the Americans: Boswell, *Life of Johnson*

Les Frites (the fried-potato-chips)

French slang for the Belgians

How much disgruntled heaviness, lameness, dampness, how much beer is there in the German intelligence.

Friedrich Nietzsche, *Twilight of the Idols*

Since both its national products, snow and chocolate, melt, the cuckoo clock was invented solely in order to give tourists something solid to remember it by.

Of Switzerland: Alan Coren

Grip your gun like a man, brother!
Let's have a crack at Holy Russia,
Mother
Russia
With her big, fat arse!

Alexander Blok, *The Twelve*, 1918

There are few virtues which the Poles do not possess and there are few errors they have ever avoided.

Winston Churchill

The French are wiser than they seem, and the Spaniards seem wiser than they are.

Francis Bacon, *Essays, Of Seeming Wise*

Holland … lies so low they're only saved by being damned.

Thomas Hood, *Up The Rhine*

The thing that impresses me most about America is the way parents obey their children.

Edward VIII (Duke of Windsor),
Look, 5 March 1957

The departure of the Wise Men from the East seems to have been on a more extensive scale than is generally supposed, for no one of that description seems to have been left behind.

Sydney Smith

~•~

I believe they manage things better across the other side. Sure God help the Irish, if it was raining soup, they'd be out with forks.

Brendan Behan, *Brendan Behan's Island*

~•~

Apart from cheese and tulips, the main product of this country is advocaat, a drink made from lawyers.

Referring to Holland: Alan Coren,
The Sanity Inspector

The ordinary women of Wales are generally short and squat, ill-favoured and nasty.

> David Mallet to Alexander Pope

Bugger Bognor!

> George V on the proposal to call the town Bognor Regis in honour of the king having convalesced there: attrib.

France is a country where the money falls apart in your hands and you can't tear the toilet paper.

> Billy Wilder: Leslie Halliwell, *Filmgoer's Book of Quotes*

The English (it must be owned) are rather a foul-mouthed nation.

William Hazlitt, *On Criticism*

~⟨●⟩~

That's this country [Ireland] all over! Not content with a contradiction in terms, it must go on to an antithesis in ideas. "Temperance Hotel"! You might as well speak of a celibate kip [brothel]!

George Tyrrell: Oliver St John Gogarty,
As I Was Going Down Sackville Street

~⟨●⟩~

In Spain, the dead are more alive than the dead of any other country in the world.

Federico Garcia Lorca,
The Duende: Theory and Divertissement

Our trouble is that we drink too much tea. I see in this the slow revenge of the Orient, which has diverted the Yellow River down our throats.

J.B. Priestley, *The Observer*, "Sayings of the Week,"
15 May 1949

Venice is like eating an entire box of chocolate liqueurs in one go.

Truman Capote, *News summaries*,
26 November 1961

London, that great cesspool into which all the loungers of the Empire are irresistably drained.

Arthur Conan Doyle, *A Study in Scarlet*

MRS ALLONBY: They say, Lady Hunstanton, that when good Americans die they go to Paris.

LADY HUNSTANTON: Indeed? And when bad Americans die, where do they go to?

LORD ILLINGWORTH: Oh, they go to America.

Oscar Wilde, *A Woman of No Importance*

Great God! This is an awful place.

Of the South Pole: Robert Falcon Scott, *Journal*

Odd's fish, they are dull and foggy.

Charles II on German princesses:
The Oxford Book of Political Anecdotes

The only good Indian is a dead Indian.

Philip Henry Sheridan at Fort Cobb: attrib.

In Ireland there's a precedent for everything. Except commonsense.

Benedict Kiely

PAUL BOURGET: Life can never be entirely dull to an American. When he has nothing else to do he can always spend a few years trying to discover who his grandfather was.

MARK TWAIN: Right, your Excellency. But I reckon a Frenchman's got a little standby for a dull time too; he can turn in and see if he can find out who his father was.

Jonathon Green,
Cassell Dictionary of Insulting Quotations

A hard-boiled city, with no more personality than a paper-clip.

Of Los Angeles: Raymond Chandler, *The Little Sister*

I look upon Switzerland as an inferior sort of Scotland.

> Sydney Smith, Letter to Lord Holland, 1815

~·❧·~

Thirty millions, mostly fools.

> Thomas Carlyle's reply to the question what was the population of England: attrib.

~·❧·~

If anyone is born a German, God has sufficiently punished him already.

> Russian saying

~·❧·~

Unmitigated noodles.

> Kaiser Wilhelm II of the English

For anything I see, foreigners are fools.
                Hugo Meynell: Boswell, *Life of Johnson*

What they all have in common, having been born in Orel [a town in Russia], is that they got out of it at the earliest opportunity.

                Alan Bennett, *Writing Home*

And, to this day, though I have kind invitations enough to visit America, I could not, even for a couple of months, live in a country so miserable as to possess no castles.

                John Ruskin writing in 1871:
                Paul Johnson, *A History of the American People*

Cusins is a very nice fellow, certainly: nobody would ever guess that he was born in Australia.

Bernard Shaw, *Major Barbara*

Life is too short to learn German.

Richard Porson: T.L. Peacock, *Gryll Grange*

Boswell: I do indeed come from Scotland, but I cannot help it ...
Johnson: That, Sir, is what a very great many of your countrymen cannot help.

Boswell, *Life of Johnson*

The English are the people of consummate cant.
Friedrich Nietzsche, *Twilight of the Idols*

America is the only nation in history which, miraculously, has gone directly from barbarism to degeneration without the usual interval of civilization.

Georges Clemenceau

Spain would be a fine country, if there were no Spaniards in it.

German saying

Poland, the doormat of Europe. Everybody steps on us.

To Be or Not to Be (film)

The Frenchman's legs are thin, his soul little; he's fickle as the wind.

Russian saying

Says he has to go to Newcastle for Christmas. I say I like Newcastle. "Why? It's all vomits and love-bites."

Alan Bennet, Writing Home

Other people have a nationality. The Irish and the Jews have a psychosis.

Brendan Behan, Richard Cork Leg, I

Englishwomen's shoes look as if they had been made by someone who had often heard shoes described, but had never seen any.

Anon

The problem with Ireland is that it's a country full of genius, but with absolutely no talent.

Hugh Leonard, *The Times*, August 1977

Shake a bridle over a Yorkshireman's grave and he will rise and steal a horse.

Lancashire saying

They are consummate hypocrites, very corrupt and lamentably deficient in stability or courage. With one gift only can they be credited on a truly heroic scale. I allude to the faculty for what a Persian might call mendacious, but I prefer to style, imaginative utterance.

George Nathaniel (later Marquis) Curzon,
Persia and The Persian Question

What a pity we have no amusements in England but vice and religion.

Sydney Smith: Hesketh Pearson, *The Smith of Smiths*

A useful phrase to learn for travelling to the Middle East:

Thank you so much for allowing me to see your marvellous gun.

Anon

The Englishwoman is so refined
She has no bosom and no behind.
Stevie Smith, *The Englishwoman*

Of course, America had often been discovered before
Columbus, but it had always been hushed up.
Oscar Wilde

There's no truth in the Dublin saying that when a
Corkman starts calling you "oul son" it's too late to
look for the knife in your back.
Brendan Behan, *Brendan Behan's Island*

Only Englishmen and dogs walk in the sun.
Italian saying

Lady Salisbury [wife of the Prime Minister] ... used to tell her friends how Lady Palmerston once said to her, "My dear, you will some day be in my position, and when you are I advise you to pay no visits at all." "So I never pay any," Lady Salisbury concluded, "except to Foreign Ambassadresses. Of course I don't include those of the South American Republics or any others of the people who live up trees."

Kenneth Rose, *Superior Person*

~°∙°~

The French tipple all the time and kill their livers, and the Scots drink in bouts and kill their neighbours.

Sir John Crofton, at a press conference launching a report "Health Education in the Prevention of Alcohol-related Problems"

~°∙°~

Every Irishman, the saying goes, has a potato in his head.

Julius Hare, *Guesses at Truth*

If possible, this visit to Naples has increased my disgust of the place and population. A more deformed, bestial-looking lot of men and women than are the Neapolitans it would be hard to match, and De Brosse's account of them holds good to this day – *C'est la plus abominable canaille, la plus dégoutante vermine qui est jamais rampé sur terre.*

Lord Ronald Leveson-Gower, diary note, c. 1886: quoted in Kenneth Rose, *Superior Person*

In point of universal sympathy with crime, the Hellenic population is not far behind the Irish. They appeared to have nothing to do but talk and pilfer.

Richard Farrer, *A Tour in Greece*, 1882

What most offends an Englishman in the heroes of French fiction is the peculiar dastardliness to women they are capable of.

George Gissing, *Commonplace Book*

I don't like the life here in New York. There is no greenery. It would make a stone sick.

Nikita Khrushchev: Robert I. Fitzhenry (ed.),
Barnes and Noble Book of Quotations

~ 🐾 ~

The people are very kindly and hospitable, but one cannot help feeling that going out is more like attending a series of servants' balls and tenants entertainments.

The Hon John Wallop, private secretary
to the governor of Tasmania, 1884:
quoted in Kenneth Rose, *Superior Person*

~ 🐾 ~

New Zealand is God's own country but it was closed the day I got there.

Robert Menzies, attrib.

In Italy the traveller notes
With great disgust the flesh of goats
Appearing on the table d'hotes;
And even this the natives spoil
By frying it in rancid oil.

Hillaire Belloc, *Cautionary Verses*

Persicos odi puer, apparatus
I hate all that Persian gear, boy.

Horace, *Odes, Bk I, 38*

It requires a surgical operation to get a joke well into a
Scotch understanding. Their only idea of wit ... is
laughing immoderately at stated intervals.

Sydney Smith: Lady Holland, *Memoir*

Chapter 3

THE ARTS

I hate all Boets and Bainters.

> George I in John Campbell,
> *Lives of the Chief Justices*

George I may have hated poets and painters but poets, painters and performing artists are pretty good at hating each other too.

I have seen, and heard, much of Cockney impudence before now; but never expected to hear a coxcomb ask two hundred guineas for flinging a pot of paint in the public's face.

On Whistler's "Nocturne in Black and Gold":
John Ruskin, *Fors Clavigera*

It is a leviathan retrieving peddles. It is a magnificent but painful hippopotamus resolved at any cost, even at the cost of its dignity, upon picking up a pea which has got into a corner of its den.

H.G. Wells, *Boon*

He had a genius for backing into the limelight.
On T.E. Lawrence: Lowell Thomas,
Lawrence of Arabia

This awful Whitman. This post-mortem poet. This poet with the private soul leaking out of him all the time. All his privacy leaking out in a sort of dribble, oozing into the universe.

Of Walt Whitman: D.H. Lawrence,
Studies in Classic American Literature

He hasn't an enemy in the world, and none of his friends like him.

Oscar Wilde on Bernard Shaw

Dr Donne's verses are like the peace of God; they pass all understanding.

James I (James VI of Scotland) on John Donne, recorded by Archdeacon Plume

This is not a novel to be tossed aside lightly. It should be thrown with great force.

Dorothy Parker, *Book Review*

… Of course, he was an old maid among novelists, even the sex obsession that lay clotted on *Ann Veronica* and *The New Machiavelli* like old white sauce was merely old maid's mania, the reaction towards the flesh of a mind too long absorbed in airships and colloids …

Rebecca West on H.G. Wells: Jane Marcus,
The Young Rebecca

A constipated swan.

Alfred de Musset of Alfred de Vigny

You write with ease to show your breeding,
But easy writing's vile hard reading.

Richard Brinsley Sheridan, *Clio's Protest*

~•~

A monstrous carbuncle on the face of a well-loved
friend.

Prince Charles's criticism of the proposed new
extension to the National Gallery, speech to the Royal
Institute of British Architects, 31 May 1984

Walpole, I thought not I should ever see
So mean a Heart as thine has proved to be;
Thou, who in Luxury nursed, beholdst with Scorn
The boy who Friendless, Fatherless, Forlorn,
Asks thy high Favour. Thou mayst call me cheat –
Say, didst thou ne'er indulge in such Deceit?
Who wrote Otranto – but I will not chide;
Scorn will repay with Scorn and Pride with Pride.
Had I the gifts of Wealth and Luxury shared –
Not poor and Mean – Walpole! Thou hadst not dared
Thus to insult – But I shall live and stand
By Rowley's side when Thou art dead and damned.

The boy poet, Thomas Chatterton, responding
to Horace Walpole who had rejected his poems
on the grounds that they were forgeries
(supposedly written by a medieval monk).
Walpole himself was the author of *The Castle of
Otranto,* which had first been published
anonymously as a translation from a fifteenth
century manuscript.

~ 80 ~

Thackeray settled like a meat-fly on whatever one had got for dinner; and made one sick of it.

John Ruskin, *Fors Clavigera*, Letter xxxi

A mad German sugar baker dancing naked in a conflagration of his own treacle.

Anonymous criticism of Thomas Lawrence's painting "Satan Summoning up his Legions"

It is a better and wiser thing to be a starved apothecary than a starved poet; so back to the shop, Mr John, back to the "plasters, pills, and ointment boxes," &c. But, for heaven's sake, young Sangrado, be a little more sparing of extenuatives and soporifics in your practice than you have been in your poetry.

John Gibson Lockhart, Review of Keats's *Endymion* in Blackwood's *Edinburgh Magazine*, 1818

Sir, there is no settling the point of precedency between a louse and a flea.

> Dr Johnson on the relative merits of two
> minor poets: Boswell, *Life of Johnson*

A weak, diffusive, weltering, ineffectual man ... a great possibility that has not realized itself. Never did I see such apparatus got ready for thinking, and so little thought.

> Thomas Carlyle of Coleridge

Two voices are there: one is of the deep;
It learns the storm cloud's thundrous melody,
Now roars, now murmurs with the changing sea,
Now bird-like pipes, now closes soft in sleep:
And one is of an old half-witted sheep
Which bleats articulate monotony,
And indicates that two and one are three,
That grass is green, lakes damp, and mountains steep
And, Wordsworth, both are thine.

J.K. Stephen, *A Sonnet*

A brain of feathers, and a heart of lead.

Alexander Pope, *The Dunciad*

When Tennyson entered the Oxford Theatre to receive his honorary degree of D.C.L., his locks hanging in admired disorder on his shoulders, dishevelled and unkempt, a voice from the gallery was heard crying out to him, "Did your mother call you early, dear?"

Julian Charles Young, *A Memoir of Charles Mayne Young with Extracts from his Son's Journal*

Why Sir, Sherry is dull, naturally dull; but it must have taken him a great deal of pains to become what we now see him. Such an excess of stupidity, Sir, is not in nature.

Dr Johnson on Thomas Sheridan:
Boswell, *Life of Johnson*

A young poet, Mr Laman Blanchard, sent Dickens a metrical contribution for *Household Words*, entitled "Orient Pearls at random strung"; but Dickens returned them with "Dear Blanchard, too much string – Yours, C.D."

Frederick Locker Lampson, *My Confidences*

~ 🐚 ~

One of the seven humbugs of Xtiandom
William Morris on Ralph Waldo Emerson

~ 🐚 ~

Publisher of a monthly journal to G.K. Chesterton (who, as is well known, was enormously fat): "Ah, Chesterton, pregnant I see."
Chesterton: "At least I don't have to bother with monthly periodicals."

Attrib.

They [the letters of Lord Chesterfield] teach the morals
of a whore and the manners of a dancing master.

Boswell, *Life of Johnson*

Drove to Regent's Park; told of Coleridge riding about
in a strange shabby dress, with I forget whom, at
Keswick, and on some company approaching them,
Coleridge offered to fall behind and pass for his
companion's servant. "No," said the other, "I am proud
of you as a friend; but, I must say, I should be ashamed
of you as a servant."

Thomas Moore, *Journals,* 4 August 1833

The first 200 pages of Ulysses … Never have I read
such tosh. As for the first two chapters we will let them
pass, but the 3rd, 4th, 5th, 6th – merely the scratchings
of pimples on the body of the bootboy at Claridges.

Of *Ulysses* by James Joyce: Virginia Woolf,
Letter to Lytton Strachey, 24 April 1922

A louse on the locks of literature.

> Alfred, Lord Tennyson of the literary critic
> Churton Collins: Ann Thwaite, Edmund Gosse

An offensive letter from a female American Catholic. I returned it to her husband with the note: "I shall be grateful if you will use whatever disciplinary means are customary in your country to restrain your wife from writing impertinent letters to men she does not know."

> Evelyn Waugh, *Diaries*, ed. Michael Davie

Swans sing before they die; 'twere no bad thing
Did certain persons die before they sing.

> Samuel Taylor Coleridge

Always looking at himself in mirrors to make sure he was sufficiently outrageous.

Enoch Powell on Byron: *Sunday Times*

I find it difficult to take much interest in a man whose father was a dragon.

Dante Gabriel Rossetti on William Morris's epic poem *Sigurd the Volsung*, 1876

The trouble, Mr Goldwyn, is that you are only interested in art, and I am only interested in money.

Telegraphed version of the outcome of a conversation between Bernard Shaw and Sam Goldwyn

I wish I was as cocksure of anything as Tom Macaulay is of everything.

Lord Melbourne on Macaulay: Earl Cowper, *Preface to Lord Melbourne's Papers*

Every other inch a gentleman.

Rebecca West of Michael Arlen: Victoria Glendinning, *Rebecca West*

Dean Inge was delighted by an angry letter he had received from a lady who disagreed with one of his articles. "I pray nightly for your death," she wrote. "It may interest you to know that in two other cases I have had great success."

Alfred Noyes, *Two Worlds for Memory*

Shockingly mad, madder than ever, quite mad.
Horace Walpole of the artist Henry Fuseli

At the time of Elizabeth Barrett Browning's death in 1861, Edward Fitzgerald wrote to a friend: "Mrs Browning's death is rather a relief to me, I must say. No more Aurora Leighs, thank God." Robert Browning learned of his comment after his death and wrote the following rejoinder:

'Twixt page and uncut page those words I read.
Some six or seven at most, and learned thereby
That you, Fitzgerald, whom by ear and eye
She never knew, "thanked God my wife was dead."
Ay, dead! And were yourself alive, good Fitz,
How to return your thanks would pass my wits.
Kicking you seems the common lot of curs –
While more appropriate greeting lends you grace:
Surely to spit there glorifies your face –
Spitting from lips once sanctified by Hers.

Robert Browning, in the *Atheneaum*, 13 July 1889

M. Cézanne must be some kind of lunatic afflicted with delirium tremens when he is painting. In fact, it is one of the weird shapes, thrown off by hashish, borrowed from a swarm of ridiculous dreams.

Anonymous French art critic

A monstrous orchid.
  Oscar Wilde on Aubrey Beardsley: Stanley Weintrab,
Aubrey Beardsley

Gibbon's style is detestable; but it is not the worst thing about him.

Samuel Taylor Coleridge, *Table Talk*

Pastel coloured sneezes …
        David Carritt on Renoir's later work: attrib.

For there is an upstart crow, beautified with our feathers, that with his tiger's heart wrapped in a player's hide, supposes he is as well able to bumbast out a blank verse as the best of you; and being an absolute Iohannes factotum, is in his own conceit the only Shake-scene in a country.

Of Shakespeare: Robert Greene, *The Groatsworth of Wit Bought with a Million of Repentance*

It is no use arguing with Johnson; for when his pistol misses fire, he knocks you down with the butt end of it.

Oliver Goldsmith of Johnson: Boswell, *Life of Johnson*

In my experience if you have to keep the lavatory door shut by extending your left leg, it's modern architecture.

Nancy Banks-Smith, *The Guardian*

You praise the firm restraint with which they write –
I'm with you there, of course:
They use the snaffle and the bit all right.
But where's the bloody horse?
Roy Campbell, *On Some South African Novelists*

Willing to wound and yet afraid to strike.
Of Joseph Addison: Alexander Pope,
Epistle to Dr Arbuthnot

An intellectual is a man who does not know how to park a bike.

Attributed to Spiro Agnew

Another damned thick, square book! Always scribble, scribble, scribble! Eh! Mr Gibbon?

Duke of Gloucester to Edward Gibbon:
Boswell, Life of Johnson

Under close scrutiny Sandburg's verse reminds us of the blobs of living jelly or plankton brought up by deep-sea dredging; it is a kind of protoplasmic poetry, lacking higher organization.

George F. Whicher in Arthur Hobson Quinn (ed.),
The Literature of the American People

The rest to some faint meaning make pretence
But Shadwell never deviates into sense
Some beams of wit on other souls may fall,
Strike through and make a lucid interval;
But Shadwell's genuine night admits no ray,
His rising fogs prevail upon the day.

    Of Thomas Shadwell: John Dryden, *MacFlecknoe*

This man [Lord Chesterfield] I thought had been a Lord among wits; but, I find, he is only a wit among Lords.

Boswell, *Life of Johnson*

Yes, he *is* good — so good one asks oneself why he is not better.

Ivy Compton-Burnett of Trollope

He will never be anything but a dauber.

Titian on Tintoretto

Monsieur Zola is determined to show that if he has not genius he can at least be dull.

Oscar Wilde on Emile Zola

Seneca writes as a boar does piss, scilicet by jerks.

Ralph Kettel: John Aubrey, *Brief Lives*

Seneca writes as a boar does piss, scilicet by jerks.

A pair of boots is in every sense better than Pushkin, because ... Pushkin is mere luxury and nonsense.

Fedor Dostoevsky, *Epokha*

... to whom Venus gave everything except beauty, and Pallas everything except wisdom.

Oscar Wilde on Margaret Sarah Fuller:
Arthur W. Brown, *Margaret Fuller*

… I am obliged to declare, Baron, that your part has not been quite suitable to you. You the representative of a crowned head, you have been as a father the pimp of your son. It would appear that all his conduct (clumsy enough, moreover) has been directed by you. It is you who probably dictated to him the wretched things that he has uttered and the silliness that he included in his writing. Like an obscene old man, you have lain in wait for my wife in every corner in order to tell her of the love of your bastard, or so he is called; and when, ill with syphilis, he was obliged to remain at home, you said that he was dying from love of her; you muttered to her: Give me back my son.

Alexander Pushkin to the Dutch Ambassador in St Petersburg, Baron George D'Anthes Heeckeren. This letter led to his fatal duel with Heeckeren's adopted son, Georges D'Anthes: Ernest J. Simmons, *Pushkin*

I enjoyed talking to her, but thought nothing of her writing. I considered her "a beautiful little knitter."
Edith Sitwell of Virginia Woolf, *Letter to G. Singleton*

Stop running those dogs on your page. I wouldn't have them peeing on my cheapest rug.
William Randolph Hearst to one of his editors about Thurber's cartoons: James Thurber, *The Years with Ross*

Of course he was a wonderful all-round man, but the act of walking round him has always tired me.
Max Beerbohm of William Morris: Max Beerbohm, *Letter to S.N. Behrman*

A vain, silly, transparent coxcomb without either solid talents or a solid nature.

J.G. Lockhart of Samuel Pepys

She is so odd a blend of Little Nell and Lady Macbeth. It is not so much the familiar phenomenon of a hand of steel in a velvet glove as a lacy sleeve with a bottle of vitriol concealed in its folds.

Of Dorothy Parker: Alexander Woollcott,
While Rome Burns

A Methodist parson in Bedlam.

Horace Walpole of Dante Alighieri

An editor is one who separates the wheat from the chaff and prints the chaff.

Adlai Stevenson on tabloid newspaper editors

The human race, to which so many of my readers belong.

G.K. Chesterton, *The Napoleon of Notting Hill*

One hates an author that's *all author* – fellows
In foolscap uniforms turned up with ink
So very anxious, clever, fine, and jealous
One don't know what to say to them, or think
Unless to puff them with a pair of bellows.

Lord Byron, *Beppo*

I have lately tried to read Shakespeare, and found it so intolerably dull that it nauseated me.

Charles Darwin, *Autobiography,* (ed.) G. de Beer

To see him fumbling with our rich and delicate language is to experience all the horror of seeing a Sèvres vase in the hands of a chimpanzee.

Of Stephen Spender: Evelyn Waugh,
The Tablet, 5 May 1951

Thank you for the manuscript. I shall lose no time in reading it.

Benjamin Disraeli's customary response to authors who sent him unsoliticited manuscripts: attrib.

Now Barrabas was a publisher.

Attributed to Thomas Campbell: Samuel Smiles,
A Publisher and his Friends

His writing bears the same relation to poetry which a Turkey carpet bears to a picture. There are words in Mr Montgomery's writing which, when disposed in certain orders and combinations, have made, and will make again, good poetry. But as they stand now they seem to be put together on principle in such a manner as to give no image of anything in the heavens above, or in the earth beneath, or in the waters under the earth.

Thomas Babington Macaulay, "Mr Robert
Montgomery's poems," *Literary Essays Contributed to
The Edinburgh Review*

Professionally he declines and falls, and as a friend he drops into poetry.

> Mr Boffin on Silas Wegg: Charles Dickens,
> *Our Mutual Friend*

He is limp and damp and milder than the breath of a cow.

> Virginia Woolf on E.M. Forster

Half song-thrush, half alligator.

> Ralph Waldo Emerson of Walt Whitman:
> Paul Johnson, *A History of the American People*

Apes are considerably preferable to Cyril.

> Virginia Woolf of Cyril Connolly: attrib.

Luminous! Oh, I meant – voluminous.

Richard Brinsley Sheridan who had referred to the "luminous philosophy of Gibbon" in his speech at the Trial of Warren Hastings: Samuel Rogers, *Table Talk*

Shaw's plays are the price we pay for Shaw's prefaces.

James Agate, *Diary,* 10 March 1933

A best-seller is the gilded tomb of a mediocre talent.

Logan Pearsall Smith, *Art and Letters*

My God, what a clumsy *olla putrida* James Joyce is! Nothing but old fags and cabbage-stumps of quotations from the Bible and the rest, stewed in the juice of deliberate, journalistic dirty-mindedness.

D.H. Lawrence, Letter to Aldous and Maria Huxley,
15 August 1928

His imagination resembled the wings of an ostrich. It enabled him to run, though not to soar.

Thomas Babington Macaulay of Dryden

It is a pretty poem, Mr Pope, but you must not call it Homer.

Richard Bentley on Pope's translation of *Homer's Iliad*:
John Hawkins (ed.), *The Works of Samuel Johnson*

Elle[Georges Sand] est bête, elle est lourde, elle est bavarde; elle a, dans les idées morales, la même profondeur de jugement et la même délicatesse de sentiment que les concierges et les filles entretenues. Que quelques hommes aient pu s'amouracher de cette latrine, c'est bien la preuve de l'abaissement des moeurs de ce siècle.

Charles Baudelaire on Georges Sand:
Jean d'Ormesson, *Une Autre Histoire de la Littérature Française*

∿⟨•⟩∿

A drowsy, frowzy poem, called the "Excursion"
Writ in a manner which is my aversion.

Of the poem by William Wordsworth:
Lord Byron, *Don Juan*

∿⟨•⟩∿

Conrad spent a day finding the *mot juste*; then killed it off.

Ford Madox Ford of Joseph Conrad:
Robert Lowell, *Notebook 1967–68*

If Shakespeare's genius had been cultivated, those beauties, which we so justly admire in him, would have been undisgraced by those extravagancies and that nonsense, with which they are so frequently accompanied.

Lord Chesterfield, *Letters to his Son*

Madame de Staël has succeeded in disguising us *both* as women.

Charles-Maurice de Talleyrand on de Staël's novel *Delphine*: Evangeline Bruce, *Napoleon and Josephine*

I can't read Ben Jonson, especially his comedies. To me he appears to move in a wide sea of glue.

Alfred Lord Tennyson:
Hallam Tennyson, *Alfred Lord Tennyson*

Gertrude Stein's prose-song is a cold, black suet pudding.

Wyndham Lewis, *Time and Western Man*

Authors are like cattle going to a fair: those of the same field can never move on without butting one another.

Walter Savage Landor, *Imaginary Conversations*

This fictional account of the day-by-day life of an English gamekeeper is still of considerable interest to outdoor-minded readers, as it contains many passages on pheasant raising, the apprehending of poachers, ways to control vermin, and other chores and duties of the professional gamekeeper. Unfortunately one is obliged to wade through many pages of extraneous material in order to discover and savour these sidelights on the management of a Midlands shooting estate, and in this reviewer's opinion this book cannot take the place of J.R. Miller's *Practical Gamekeeping*.

Anonymous review of D.H. Lawrence,
Lady Chatterley's Lover: attributed to *Field and Stream*

You know I can't stand Shakespeare's plays, but yours are even worse.

Leo Tolstoy to Anton Chekhov after seeing Uncle Vanya: P.P. Gnedich, *Kniga Zhnizni Vospominaniya*

Four happy publishers
Out on a spree.
Someone had to pay the bill
And then there were three.

> Wendy Cope, *Two Hand-Rhymes for Grown-ups*

A pretentious fad-chaser ... the pom-pom girl of American letters.

> Edward Abbey of Tom Wolfe: attrib.

His attitude to most accredited sources of pleasure would make Scrooge seem unduly frolicsome.

> John Carey of Philip Larkin, *Sunday Times*, 1983

How odious all authors are, and how doubly so to each other!

Henry Fox, Lord Holland, Letter, 3 January 1821

Your solemn mug is so like an old peasant woman's arse that all it asks for is to be kicked.

Alexander Pushkin, Epigram to Ivan Lanov:
David Magarshack, *Pushkin*

The Llama is a woolly sort of fleecy hairy goat,
With an indolent expression and an undulating throat
Like an unsuccessful literary man.

Hillaire Belloc, *Cautionary Verses*

Johnny Keats's piss-a-bed poetry.
> Lord Byron, Letter to John Murray,
> 12 October 1818

The original Greek is of great use in elucidating Browning's translation of the Agamemnon.
> Robert Yelverton Tyrrell:
> Ulick O'Connor, *Oliver St John Gogarty*

If Goethe is a god, I am sure I'd rather go to the other place.
> William Makepeace Thackeray: Ann Monsarrat,
> *Thackeray, An Uneasy Victorian*

A man who so much resembled a Baked Alaska – sweet, warm and gungy on the outside, hard and cold within.

> Of C.P. Snow: Francis King,
> *Yesterday Came Suddenly*

People who like this sort of thing will find this the sort of thing they like.

> Abraham Lincoln's review of a book: G.W.E. Russell,
> *Collections and Recollections*

All newspaper and journalistic activity is an intellectual brothel from which there is no retreat.

> Leo Tolstoy, Letter to Prince V.P. Meshchersky,
> 22 August 1871

It is the process of painting which is repellent; to force from little tubes of lead a glutinous flamboyance and to defile, with the hair of a camel therein steeped, taut canvas, is hardly the diversion for a gentleman.

    Max Beerbohm deploring the fact that Count d'Orsay
       was a portrait painter: in Ellen Moers, *The Dandy*

C'est la vache bretonne de la littérature.

    Jules Renard of Georges Sand: Jean D'Ormesson,
       Une Autre Histoire de la Littérature Française

Hot, envious, noisy, proud, the scribbling fry
Burn, hiss and bounce, waste paper, stink, and die.

    Edward Young, *The Love of Fame*

The covers of this book are too far apart.
Ambrose Bierce: attrib.

The floods of tepid soap and water which under the name of novels are being vomited forth in England, seem to me, by contrast [with French fiction], to do little honour to our race.
Henry James, Letter, 21 February 1884

From the moment I picked up your book until I laid it down, I was convulsed with laughter. Some day I intend reading it.

Groucho Marx

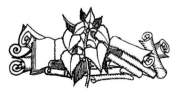

I called him a wrinkled and toothless baboon, who, first hoisted in notoriety on the shoulders of Carlyle, now spits and splutters on a filthier platform of his own finding and fouling.

> Algernon Charles Swinburne of
> Ralph Waldo Emerson: Evan Charteris,
> *Life and Letters of Sir Edmund Gosse*

Yea, marry, now it is somewhat, for now it is rhyme; before it was neither rhyme nor reason.

> Sir Thomas More on reading a dull book put into
> verse by a friend of his: Francis Bacon,
> *Apophthegms New and Old*

Rudyard the dud yard ...

> Of Rudyard Kipling: Ezra Pound,
> *Poems of Alfred Venison: Alf's Fourth Bit*

Poets arguing about modern poetry; jackals snarling over a dried-up well.

Cyril Connolly, *The Unquiet Grave*

Is not a patron, My Lord, one who looks with unconcern on a man struggling for life in the water and, when he has reached ground, encumbers him with help? The notice which you have been pleased to take of my labours, had it been early, had been kind; but it has been delayed till I am indifferent and cannot enjoy it, till I am solitary and cannot impart it, till I am known and do not want it.

Dr Johnson's letter to Lord Chesterfield on the occasion of the publication of his *Dictionary*:
Boswell, *Life of Johnson*

"By God," quod he, "for pleynly, at a word,
Thy drasty rhymyng is nat worth a toord!"

Geoffrey Chaucer, *Sir Thopas*

Wordsworth, a stupid man, with a decided gift for portraying nature in vignettes, never yet ruined anyone's morals, unless, perhaps, he has driven some susceptible persons to crime in a very fury of boredom.

Ezra Pound, *Future September*

The actor, John Barrymore, annoyed by a plague of coughing in the audience during the first act, produced a fish from under his coat at the beginning of the second, saying: "Chew on that, you walruses, while the rest of us get on with the libretto."

John Train, *Wit*

Difficult do you call it, Sir. I wish it were impossible!

Dr Johnson on the performance of a celebrated violinist: in William Seward, *Supplement to the Anecdotes of Distinguished Persons*

The first night of Victor Hugo's romantic tragedy *Hernani* provoked a storm of protest from the classicists in the audience, who laughed and hissed throughout the play. Hugo's supporters gave as good as they got. "Madame," said one of them, "you do wrong to laugh; you show your teeth."

Linda Kelly, *The Young Romantics*

If white bread could sing it would sound like Olivia Newton John.

Anon

Richard Cumberland was a well-known figure in his time. He was the author of fifty plays, one of which *The West Indian* had almost the status of a classic. But, despite his achievements he was ludicrously envious of other writers. He was said to have been so jealous of *The School for Scandal* that when he saw it with his children during its first run he pinched his children to stop them from laughing.

Sheridan having been told of this long afterwards, said, "It was very ungrateful in Cumberland to have been displeased with his poor children for laughing at my comedy; for I went the other night to see his tragedy, and laughed at it from beginning to end."

Linda Kelly, Richard Brinsley Sheridan

She ran the whole gamut of emotions from A to B.

Dorothy Parker of Katharine Hepburn
at a Broadway first night: attrib.

That's a lot to see buggers jump.
  Nigel Bruce, commenting on the cost of ballet tickets

A trip through a sewer in a glass-bottomed boat.
  Wilson Mizner of Hollywood

The great Shakespearian actor, John Phillip Kemble, interrupted by the persistent squalling of a child in the audience, stepped forward and announced in tragic tones: "Ladies and Gentlemen, if the play is not stopped, the child cannot possibly go on."

  Attrib.

Tosca, that shabby little shocker …
  Joseph Kerman, *Opera as Drama*

Henry James was complaining to us that Ellen Terry had asked him to write a play for her, and now that he had done so, and read it to her, had refused it. My wife, desiring to placate, asked: "Perhaps she did not think the part suited to her?" Henry James turned upon us both, and with resonance and uplifting voice replied: "Think? Think? How should the poor, toothless, chattering hag THINK?" The sudden outpouring of improvised epithets had a most extraordinary effect. A crescendo on "toothless" and then on "chattering" and then on "hag" – and "think" delivered with the trumpet of an elephant.

> *Letters and Diaries: John Bailey, 1864–1931:*
> Edited by his wife

Beatlemania is like the frenzied dancing and shouting of voodoo worshippers and the howls and bodily writhings of converts among primitive evangelical sects in the southern states of America.

> Dr F. Casson in *The Times*, 1963

Once after he [Caruso] had sung a duet with a celebrated soprano, more noted for her beauty than her voice, I asked how he liked her singing. "I don't know," he replied, "I never heard her."

Dorothy Caruso, *Enrico Caruso*

Wagner has lovely moments, but awful quarters of an hour.

Rossini in a letter to Emile Nauman, April 1867

I encouraged Yeats to speak about the actress Mrs. Pat Campbell, who had played in his *Dierdre*. He described her as having "an ego like a raging tooth," and spoke of her habit of "throwing tantrums" at rehearsals. On one occasion after a particularly wild "tantrum" she walked to the footlights and peered out at Yeats, who was pacing up and down the stalls of the Abbey Theatre. "I'd give anything to know what you're thinking," shouted Mrs. Pat. "I'm thinking," replied Yeats, "of the master of a wayside Indian railway station who sent a message to his Company's headquarters saying: 'Tigress on the line: wire instructions.'"

Gabriel Fallon, *Sean O'Casey: The Man I Knew*

~§~

Lillian Gish may be a charming person, but she is not Ophelia. She comes on stage as if she had been sent for to sew rings on the new curtains.

Mrs Campbell on a fellow actress:
Margot Peters, *Mrs Pat*

A glorified bandmaster!

> Sir Thomas Beecham of Toscanini: in Neville
> Cardus, *Sir Thomas Beecham*

The only ism Hollywood believes in is plagiarism.

> Dorothy Parker

OSWALD: What dost thou know me for?
KENT: A knave, a rascal, an eater of broken meats; a base, proud, shallow, beggarly, three-suited, hundred-pound, filthy, worsted-stocking knave; a lily-liver'd, action-taking knave; a rogue; one-trunk inheriting slave; one that wouldst be a bawd, in a way of good service, and art nothing but the composition of a knave, beggar, coward, pandar, and the son and heir of a mongrel bitch; one whom I will beat into clamorous whining if thou deniest the least syllable of thy addition.

> William Shakespeare, *King Lear*

W.H. Auden was talking to Stravinsky about Benjamin Britten's opinion of his opera *The Rake's Progress*. Auden repeated his story about Benjamin Britten liking the opera very much: "Everything except the music."

Robert Craft, *Stravinsky, Chronicle of a Friendship*

Another dirty shirt-tail actor from New York.

Hedda Hopper of the film star James Dean

The musical equivalent of St Pancras Station.

Sir Thomas Beecham on Elgar's Symphony in A Flat

A plumber's idea of Cleopatra.

W.C. Fields of the film star Mae West

The young tenor di Stefano appeared at the Theatre Colon, in Buenos Aires, in the same season as Gigli, and was disturbed to find that on one of the many bills, his name appeared in larger type than Gigli's. He told the great man at once this apparent slight was none of his doing and that it distressed him to see himself given such precedence. "Don't worry, my young friend," Gigli loftily told him, "as soon as the public hear us both, they will realize which billing is correct."

Ivor Newton, *At the Piano*

Sergei Rachmaninov's immortalising totality was his scowl. He was a six-and-a-half foot scowl.

Igor Stravinsky

Like *Parsifal* but without the jokes.

Thomas Beecham on Hans Pfitzner's opera *Palestrino*: attrib.

She has only two expressions – joy and indigestion.

Dorothy Parker of the film star Marion Davies

Meyerbeer ... used to send two elegantly dressed gentlemen to every performance of Rossini's operas. It was the duty of these two gentlemen to sit in well-exposed box seats and fall fast asleep fifteen minutes after the curtain rose. At the end of the opera they had to be wakened by the usher. Regular opera subscribers were familiar with these "sommeilleurs de Meyerbeer." For a performance of *Semiramis*, Rossini sent two tickets to Meyerbeer himself. "Please do me the favour," he wrote, "of using these tickets yourself. The box is visible from all parts of the house. The chairs are comfortable. Shortly before the end of the performance I shall have you waked. Your true admirer, G. Rossini."

George R. Marek, *A Front Seat at the Opera*

The odd and pleasant taste of a pink sweet filled with snow.

Claude Debussy of Grieg's music

The poet Samuel Rogers once teased Sheridan about his admiration for the great tragic actress, Mrs Sidddons, and wondered he did not make open love to her.

"To her," said Sheridan, "to that magnificent and appalling creature! I should as soon have thought of making love to the Archbishop of Canterbury."

Samuel Rogers, Table Talk

The kind of opera that starts at six o'clock and after it has been going three hours you look at your watch and it says 6.20.

David Randolph of the opera Parsifal: Frank Muir,
Frank Muir Book

The Devil damn thee black, thou cream-fac'd loon!
Where gott'st thou that goose look?

Macbeth to a servant:
William Shakespeare, *Macbeth*

~·🐚·~

I had a great deal of say ... but the producer didn't
have a great deal of listen.

Douglas Adams about the television adaptation of
The Hitch-Hiker's Guide to the Galaxy: Stan Nicholls
(ed.), *Wordsmiths of Wonder*

~·🐚·~

After a royal command concert at Windsor Castle at
which a number of distinguished musicians
performed, she [Nellie Melba] turned to the Lord
Chamberlain and complained in a loud voice, "What a
dreadful concert this would have been if I hadn't
come ..."

Of Dame Nellie Melba: Rupert Christiansen,
Prima Donna

In that wig you could play Lassie.

The Mirror Crack'd (film)

When the curtain fell, I was asked by all my acquaintances how I liked the opera? My answer flew from my lips like lightning: "It is paradise for the eyes, and hell for the ears."

Of French opera: Carlo Goldoni, *Memoirs*

Television is an invention that permits you to be entertained in your living room by people you wouldn't have in your home.

David Frost, *David Frost Review*, CBS TV, 1971

... atrociously stupid. I was thinking of something else the whole time she was jugulating away ...

William Makepeace Thakeray of a performance by Jenny Lind "the Swedish Nightingale": Stephen Brook (ed.), *Opera, A Penguin Anthology*

My dear fellow a unique evening! I wouldn't have left a turn unstoned.

Arthur Wimperis giving his opinion of a vaudeville show: E. Short, *Fifty Years of Vaudeville*

Her rendition was a howling success.

Louis A. Safian

Brahms is just like Tennyson, an extraordinary musician, with the brains of a third rate village policeman.

> Bernard Shaw, Letter to Pakenham Beatty,
> 4 April 1893

She looks like she combs her hair with an egg beater.

> Louella Parsons of Joan Collins

An unreconstructed dinosaur.

> Budd Schulberg of Harry Cohn

Foote is quite impartial, for he tells lies of everybody.
Of the actor Samuel Foote:
Boswell, *Life of Johnson*

– It's [Los Angeles] so clean out here.
– That's because they don't throw their garbage away.
They turn it into television shows.
Woody Allen, *Annie Hall*

The audience shouted out "Intellectual rot" and were soon in a state of riot. When the dead seagull was brought in, a wit sitting next to a friend of Chekhov's shouted out, "Why does this Apollonsky [the actor who played Treplev] carry a dead duck about with him."
The first night of *The Seagull* by Chekhov:
V.S. Pritchett, *Chekhov, A Spirit Set Free*

... most ballets would be quite delightful if it were not for the dancing.

M. Bateman, *This England, selections from the New Statesman*

As the La Scala company in 1865 were rehearsing a new opera, with the composer in attendance, the impresario burst in, stopped the orchestra, and said he wanted to rehearse a different opera with a tenor who was making an emergency debut the next day. The composer shouted, wept, and stamped his feet at the "murder of Art"; the baritone shouted that he would not rehearse two operas in one evening; the impresario shouted back in dialect, "I'm paying and I give the orders." After an exchange of insults the impresario slapped the baritone; in the resulting scrum the conductor fell down, a drunken inspector from the supervisory board fell on top of him, the chorus intervened, and the baritone and the bass came to blows over the soprano, with the one grabbing the other in the "reproductive region." The impresario ran off.

John Rosselli, *Singers of Italian Opera*

His life was a fifty-year-old trespass against good taste.

Leslie Mallory of Erroll Flynn

There's only one explanation for that voice – he gargles with ground glass.

Louis A. Safian

Too many notes.

Joseph II on Mozart's music: attrib.

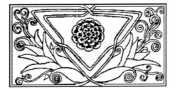

It [a production of Brecht's *The Days of the Communal*] has the depth of a cracker motto, the drama of a dial-a-recipe service and the eloquence of a conversation between a speak-your-weight machine and a whoopee cushion.

Bernard Levin, *Sunday Times*, 1977

His [Stravinsky's] music used to be original. Now it is aboriginal.

Ernest Newman, *Musical Times*, 1921

John, every day you act worse, but today, you're acting like tomorrow.

Roberta (film)

Wagner's music is better than it sounds.

Mark Twain: attrib.

Once, passing a suite at the Savoy Hotel, London, while Melba was practising, Tetrazzini turned to Mrs Kate Butler, the Savoy's superintendent, and asked, "Have you many cats in your lovely hotel?"

Of Dame Nellie Melba:
John Hetherington, *Melba*

Did you go to a rock concert? How was it? Was it heavy? Did it achieve total heavyocrity?

Woody Allen, *Annie Hall* (film)

The public is a thick-skinned beast and you have to keep whacking away on its hide to let it know you're there.

> Walt Whitman: Paul Johnson,
> *A History of the American People*

Thou Mimic of Cibber – Of Garrick, thou Ape
Thou Fop in Othello! thou Cypher in Shape!
Thou trifle in Person! thou puppet in Voice!
Thou farce of a Player! thou Rattle for Boys!
Thou Mongrell! thou diry face Harlequin Thing!
Thou Puff of bad Paste! thou Ginger-bread King!

> Anonymous: W.R. Chetwood,
> *A General History of the Stage*

She was a singer who had to take any note above A
with her eyebrows.

   Of Montague Glass: Frank Muir, *Frank Muir Book*

One of the thousand reasons I quit going to the
theatre when I was about twenty was that I resented
like hell filing out of the theatre just because some
playwright was forever slamming down his silly
curtain.

J.D. Salinger

Schmucks with Underwoods.

Jack Warner on scriptwriters: attrib.

House Beautiful is Play Lousy.

Dorothy Parker, *New Yorker Review*, 1933

Chapter 4

❧

THE WAR OF THE SEXES

Hell to ships, hell to men, hell to cities.
(Literally "Ship-destroyer, man-destroyer, city-
destroyer.")
        Of Helen of Troy: Aeschylus, *Agamemnon*

*The war of the sexes is as old as history; the struggle
continues.*

Sir! This lady is my wife. You should be ashamed.
If this lady is your wife, *you* should be ashamed.

Groucho Marx in *A Night in Casablanca* (film)

A woman's preaching is like a dog's walking on his hinder legs. It is not done well, but you are surprised to find it done at all.

Boswell, *Life of Johnson*

Bessie Braddock: Winston, you are drunk, horribly drunk.
Winston Churchill: And Madam, you are ugly, terribly ugly, but in the morning I shall be sober.

J.L. Lane (ed.), *Sayings of Winston Churchill*

Someone mentioned that a young Scot was about to marry an Irish widow, twice his age and more than twice his size.

"Going to marry her!" cried Sydney Smith, "going to marry her! Impossible! You mean a part of her; he could not marry her all himself. It would be a case, not of bigamy, but trigamy; the neighbourhood or the magistrates should interfere. There is enough of her to furnish wives for a whole parish. One man marry her! it is monstrous! You might people a colony with her, or give an assembly with her, or perhaps take your morning's walk round her, always provided there were freequent resting-places, and you were in rude health. I once was rash enough to try walking round her before breakfast, but only got half-way and gave it up exhausted. Or you might read the Riot Act and disperse her; in short, you might do anything with her but marry her."

Sydney Smith: in David Cecil, *Library Looking-Glass*

~ ❦ ~

Certain women should be struck regularly, like gongs.
Noel Coward, *Private Lives*

They're as companionable as a cat and a goldfish.

Anon

The king found her so different from her picture …
that … he swore they had bought him a Flanders
mare.

Henry VIII and Anne of Cleves: Tobias Smollett,
Complete History of England

Your teeth are like stars; they come out at night!

Anon

That hyena in petticoats, Mrs Wollstonecraft.
Horace Walpole of Mary Wollstonecraft, Letter to
Hannah More, 26 January 1795

Nancy Astor: If I were your wife I would put poison in your coffee!

Winston Churchill: And if I were your husband I would drink it.

Consuelo Vanderbilt Balsan, *Glitter and Gold*

A certain Mrs Dumby challenged Dr Johnson to make up an impromptu rhyme on her name. He wrote the following:

You make a mistake
If you think I can't make
A rhyme on your name, Mrs Dumby.
If your face is so fair
When exposed to the air
How much fairer by far
Must your – be.

Attrib.

She looked a million dollars, I must admit, even if in well-used notes.

Angela Carter, *Wise Children*

The only solid and lasting peace between a man and his wife is, doubtless, a separation.

Lord Chesterfield, *Letters to his Son*

Mrs Hull of Sherbourne was brought to bed yesterday of a dead child, some weeks before she expected, owing to a fright. I suppose she happened to look at her husband.

Jane Austen, Letter, 27 October 1748

But – Oh! Ye lords of ladies intellectual,
Inform us truly, have they not hen-pecked you all?

Byron, *Don Juan*

She wore one of those dresses made at home and repented at leisure.

Saki (Hector Hugh Munro)

I wouldn't marry you to keep warm on an iceberg!
Roland Young to Lillian Roth in *Madam Satan* (film)

BISHOP: Who is it that sees and hears all we do, and before whom even I am but as a crushed worm?
PAGE: The Missus, my Lord.

Punch, 1880

When once a woman has given you her heart, you can never get rid of the rest of her body.

Sir John Vanbrugh, The Relapse

She has discovered the secret of perpetual middle age.

Oscar Levant

O! she misused me past the endurance of a block: an oak but with one green leaf on it would have answered her: my very visor began to assume life and scold with her. She told me ... that I was duller than a great thaw; huddling jest upon jest with such impossible conveyance upon me, that I stood like a man at a mark, with a whole army shooting at me. She speaks poinards, and every word stabs: if her breath were as terrible as her terminations there were no living near her; she would infect to the north star. I would not marry her, though she were endowed with all that Adam had left him before he transgressed: she would have made Hercules have turned spit, yea, and have cleft his club to make the fire too ...

Benedick of Beatrice: William Shakespeare, *Much Ado About Nothing*

~☙~

Courtship to marriage, as a very witty prologue to a very dull play.

William Congreve, *The Old Bachelor*

She's far from her own sylph.

Anon

Publish and be damned!
Duke of Wellington, replying to Harriet Wilson who had threatened to expose him in her memoirs.

She did not so much cook as assasinate food.
Of the writer Storm Jameson: Anon

Nature played a cruel trick on her by giving her a waxed mustache.

Alan Bennett

Remember thee! Remember thee!
Till Lethe quench life's burning stream
Remorse and Shame shall cling to thee,
And haunt thee like a feverish dream!

Remember thee! Aye, doubt it not.
Thy husband too shall think of thee:
By neither shall thou be forgot,
Thou false to him, thou fiend to me!

> Lord Byron to Lady Caroline Lamb,
> who continued to pursue him with jealous scenes
> after their much publicized love affair

At last she sleeps alone.

> Epitaph on a famously promiscuous actress:
> Robert Benchley

Old blondes never fade, like her, they just dye away.

> Anon

The only really masterful noise a man makes in a house is the noise of his key, when he is still on the landing, fumbling for the lock.

Colette

A woman is like an elephant – I like to look at 'em, but I wouldn't want to own one.

W.C. Fields in *Mississippi* (film)

Actually, I don't dislike women, I merely distrust them. The twinkle in the eye and the arsenic in the soup.

The Private Life of Sherlock Holmes (film)

She's so deliciously low, so horribly dirty ... I shall make a duchess of this draggle-tailed guttersnipe.

Professor Higgins of Eliza Doolittle in
My Fair Lady (film)

I call her a ghastly girl because she was a ghastly girl. The Woosters are chivalrous, but they can speak their minds. A droopy, soupy, sentimental exhibit, with melting eyes and a cooing voice and the most extraordinary views on such things as stars and rabbits. I remember her telling me once that rabbits were gnomes in attendance on the Fairy Queen, and that the stars were God's daisy chain. Perfect rot, of course. They're nothing of the sort.

P.G. Wodehouse, *The Code of the Woosters*

That woman speaks eight languages and she can't say "no" in any of them.

Dorothy Parker

~ ❧ ~

The nicest thing I can say about Frances Farmer is that she is unbearable.

William Wyler: attrib.

~ ❧ ~

She looks like a million dollars – after taxes.

Anon

~ ❧ ~

Sure, deck your lower limbs in pants;
Yours are the limbs, my sweeting.
You look divine as you advance –
Have you seen yourself retreating.

Ogden Nash, *What's the Use*

But supposing the child had your brains and my looks.
Bernard Shaw's reply to the actress Mrs Patrick
Campbell who had said that with her looks and his
brains they could have a splendid child: attrib.

Her only flair is in her nostrils.

Pauline Kael

I wouldn't marry you if you were young, which you
can't be, if you were honest, but you never were, or if
you were about to die tomorrow, which is too much to
hope for.

March of the Wooden Soldiers (film)

Bloody men are like bloody buses
You wait for about a year
And as soon as one approaches your stop
Two or three others appear.

Wendy Cope, *Bloody Men*

Boiled down to essentials, she is a plain mortal with large feet.

Herbert Kretzner of Greta Garbo

I rather think of having a career of my own.

Arthur James Balfour, when asked whether he was going to marry Margot Tennant: Margot Asquith, *Autobiography*

She's what we used to call a suicide blonde — dyed by
her own hand.

Saul Bellow

～ ﹛🐾﹜～

… i met a slick looking tom
    out at one of these long island
    spotless towns
    he fell for me hard
he slipped me into the
    pantry and just as we had got
    the ice-box door open and were
    about to sample the cream
    in comes his mistress
    why fluffy she says to this slicker
the idea of you making
    friends with a horrid creature like that
    and what did fluffy do
    stand up for me like a gentleman
    make good on all the promises
    with which he had lured me
    into his house
    not he the dirty slob

he pretended he did not know me
he turned upon me and attacked me
to make good with his boss
you mush faced bum I said
and clawed a piece out of his ear
i am a lady archy
always a lady
but an aristocrat will
always resent an insult ...

Don Marquis, *archy and mehitabel*

There is nothing so similar to one poodle dog as another poodle dog, and that goes for women too.

Pablo Picasso

A woman whose face looked as if it had been made of sugar and someone had licked it.

Bernard Shaw of the dancer Isadora Duncan

The comfortable estate of widowhood is the only hope that keeps up a wife's spirits.

John Gay, *The Beggar's Opera*

The trouble with [Ian] Fleming is that he gets off with women, because he can't get on with them.

Rosamund Lehmann: quoted in J. Pearson,
The Life of Ian Fleming

Oscar Wilde to Sarah Bernhardt: Do you mind if I smoke?
Sarah Bernhardt to Oscar Wilde: I don't care if you burn.

Attrib.

ANTHONY to CLEOPATRA: … and let
Patient Octavia plough thy visage up
With her prepared nails.

> William Shakespeare, *Anthony and Cleopatra*

She has not only kept her lovely figure, she's added so
much to it.

> Bob Fosse

Here lies my wife.
Here let her lie!
Now she's at rest. And so am I.

> John Dryden, (proposed) Epitaph for his Wife

A man ... is so in the way in the house!

Elizabeth Gaskell, *Cranford*

They call her "Appendix" – if you take her out once,
that's enough.

Anon

Mrs Pugh

 Persons with manners do not read at table.

First Voice

 says Mrs Pugh. She swallows a digestive tablet as big as a horse-pill, washing it down with clouded peasoup water.

[Pause]

Mrs Pugh

 Some persons were brought up in pigsties.

Mr Pugh

 Pigs don't read at table, dear.

First Voice

 Bitterly she flicks dust from the broken cruet. It settles on the pie in a thin gnat-rain.

Mr Pugh

 Pigs can't read, my dear.

Mrs Pugh

 I know one who can.

Dylan Thomas, *Under Milk Wood*

Her motto is: "Dough or die."

Anon

This prison is known as the first brothel in Paris and you are all a lot of whores!

Prisoner administrator of the Les Carmes jail to newly-arrived women prisoners during the French Revolution: Evangeline Bruce, *Napoleon and Josephine*

~ 165 ~

LYSANDER: [To Hermia] Hang off, thou cat, thou burr!
vile thing, let loose,
Or I will shake thee from me like a serpent.
HERMIA: Why are you grown so rude? What change is
    this,
Sweet love, –
LYSANDER: Thy love! out, tawny Tartar, out!
Out loathed medicine! hated poison, hence!
HERMIA: Do you not jest? …
… Am I not Hermia? Are you not Lysander?
I am as fair now as I was erewhile.
Since night you lov'd me; yet, since night you left me:
Why, then you left me,– O, the gods forbid! –
In earnest, shall I say?
LYSANDER: Ay, by my life;
And never did desire to see thee more.
Therefore be out of hope, of question, doubt;
Be certain, nothing truer: 'tis no jest,
That I do hate thee and love Helena.
HERMIA: O me! you juggler! you canker-blossom! …

William Shakespeare,
A Midsummer Night's Dream

Men are generally more careful of the breed of their horses and dogs than of their children.

William Penn, *Some Fruits of Solitude,*
in Reflections and Maxims relating to the conduct of
Humane Life

She married a dreamer, and found he's just a sleeper.

Anon

Emily, I have a little confession to make. I really am a horse-doctor, but marry me and I'll never look at another horse.

Groucho Marx, *A Day at the Races* (film)

Many a man has fallen in love with a girl in a light so dim he would not have chosen a suit by it.

Maurice Chevalier: attrib.

PISTOL: I know you, Mistress Dorothy.

DOLL TEARSHEET: Away, you cut-purse rascal! you filthy bung, away! By this wine, I'll thrust my knife in your mouldy chaps an you play the saucy cuttle with me. Away, you bottle-ale rascal! you basket-hilt stale juggler, you! …

William Shakespeare, *Henry IV*

She sure has the gift of grab.

Anon

Will you take your clammy hands off my chair? You have the touch of a love-starved cobra.

The Man Who Came to Dinner (film)

～٤◖～

PETRUCHIO: Nay, come, Kate, come; you must not look so sour.
KATHARINA: It is my fashion when I see a crab.
PETRUCHIO: Why, here's no crab, and therefore look not sour.
KATHARINA: There is, there is.
PETRUCHIO: Then show it me.
KATHARINA: Had I a glass, I would.
PETRUCHIO: What, you mean my face?

William Shakespeare, *The Taming of the Shrew*

～٤◖～

She wanted a mink coat, so he got her a trap and a gun.

Anon

Counsel: But is the jury to understand, Mr Haddock, that in your opinion the highbrow is necessarily of the feminine gender?

Witness: Of course. It is one of the special diseases of women.

A.P. Herbert, *Uncommon Law*

If all the girls at a Yale prom were laid end-to-end, I wouldn't be at all surprised.

Dorothy Parker

Men call her "Sugar" and end up paying a lump sum.

Anon

An unhappy alternative is before you, Elizabeth. From this day you must be a stranger to one of your parents. Your mother will never see you again if you do not marry Mr Collins, and I will never see you again if you do.

Mr Bennet to his daughter:
Jane Austen, *Pride and Prejudice*

~❦~

She's sticking to him through thick and gin.

Anon

~❦~

Do you know why God withheld the sense of humour from women? That we may love you instead of laughing at you.

Mrs Patrick Campbell to a man:
M. Peters, *The Life of Mrs Pat*

He married her for her looks, but not the kind he's getting now.

Louis A. Safian

Mad, bad, and dangerous to know.

Lady Caroline Lamb, of Byron, in her journal

She's all preaches and scream.

Anon

Mary Jane Canary was a dear and selfless woman, but she looked like an unmade bed.

Sunset (film)

Polly: Then all my sorrows are at an end.
Mrs Peachum: A mighty likely speech, in truth, for a wench who is just married.

John Gay, *The Beggar's Opera*

That monstrous animal, a husband and wife.

Henry Fielding, *Tom Jones*

All she wants is to see his name just once in the obituary column

Anon

Buy old masters. They fetch a better price than old mistresses.

Lord Beaverbrook: attrib.

You know, you wouldn't be a bad looking dame ... if it wasn't for your face.

Hold Your Man (film)

A man is like a phonograph with half-a-dozen records. You soon get tired of them all; and yet you have to sit at table whilst he reels them off to every visitor.

Bernard Shaw, *Getting Married*

Late last night I slew my wife,
Stretched her on the parquet flooring;
I was loathe to take her life,
But I had to stop her snoring!

Harry Graham, *When Grandma fell off the Boat*

The majority of husbands remind me of an orangutang trying to play the violin.

Honore de Balzac, *The Physiology of Marriage*

～❦～

When she wears slacks she reveals stern facts.

Louis A. Safian

～❦～

The sniffs I get from the ink of women are always fey, old-bat, Quaintsy, Gaysy, tiny, too dykily psychotic, crippled, creepish fashionable, frigid, outer-Baroque, maquille in mannequin's whimsey, or else bright and stillborn.

Norman Mailer, *Advertisements for Myself*

Getting better acquainted with him is like making a pet out of a polecat.

Calamity Jane (film)

There's nothing so stubborn as a man when you want him to do something.

Jean Giraudoux, *The Madwoman of Chaillot*

But of all the plagues, the greatest is untold,
The book-learned wife in Greek and Latin bold,
The critic-dame, who at her table sits,
Homer and Virgil quotes, and wrights their wits.

John Dryden, translation of Juvenal, *Satires*

His absence makes her heart go wander.

Anon

Men at most differ as heaven and earth
But, women, worst and best, as heaven and hell.

> Alfred, Lord Tennyson, *Idylls of the King*

We wouldn't be caught dead with men. Rough, hairy beasts. Eight hands. And they all want just one thing from a girl.

> *Some Like it Hot* (film)

Her frocks are built in Paris, but she wears them with a strong English accent.

> Saki [H.H. Munro]

A fellah like that reminds me of a side of pork: streak of fat, streak of lean, streak of good, streak of mean.

> *Honky Tonk* (film)

Women upset everything. When you let them into your life, you find that the woman is driving at one thing and you're driving at another.

Bernard Shaw, *Pygmalion*

A good marriage would be between a blind wife and a deaf husband.

Michel de Montaigne, *Essays*

I sometimes think that God, in creating man, somewhat overestimated his ability.

Oscar Wilde

She has switchboard hips – every line is busy.

Louis A. Safian

❦

As brief as a husband's kiss.

Spanish saying

❦

Can't you read? The score says *con amore*, and what are you doing? You are playing like married men.

Arturo Toscanini criticising the playing of an Austrian orchestra during a rehearsal: attrib.

❦

He brings home the bacon and she burns it.

Anon

As from a bear a man would run for life.
So fly I from her that would be my wife.
William Shakespeare, *A Comedy of Errors*

Never let one man worry your mind. Find 'em, fool
'em and forget 'em.
Mae West in *I'm No Angel* (film)

Rannveig said: You are an evil woman, and your
shame will long be remembered.
Penguin Classics, *Njal's Saga* (translated by
Magnus Magnusson and Hermann Palsson)

Most of us grow up to be the kind of men our mothers
warned us against.
Brendan Behan

Eric: Philippa happens to be very good with children.
Helen: Presumably why she lives with you.
Alan Ayckbourn, *Ten Times Table*

A singular old deevil who talks as big as St Paul's.
William Makepeace Thackeray on Mrs Shawe
his mother-in-law: Ann Monsarrat,
Thackeray, An Uneasy Victorian

The more I see of men, the more I admire dogs.
Marquise de Sévigné: attrib.

O, she is the antidote to desire.
William Congreve, *The Way of the World*

Foul words is but foul wind, wind is but foul breath, and foul breath is noisome; therefore I will depart unkissed.

Beatrice to Benedick:
William Shakespeare, *Much Ado About Nothing*

Chapter 5

POLITICS

The Right Honourable Gentleman is indebted
to his memory for his jests and his imagination
for his facts.
Richard Brinsley Sheridan to Henry Dundas
in the House of Commons

Political insults range from the suave to the scurrilous.

You look like an Easter Island statue with an arse full of razor blades.

> Paul Keating to Malcolm Fraser

The vice-presidency of America isn't worth a pitcher of warm piss.

> John Nance Garner to the then Vice-President
> Lyndon B. Johnson

Hitler
Has only got one ball
Himmler
Has two, but one is rather small
And Goebbels
Has no balls
At all.

> World War II song, sung to the tune
> of "Colonel Bogey"

Henry V's indignation at receiving the gift of tennis balls from the King of France:

FIRST AMBASSADOR TO FRANCE: Thus then, in few.
Your highness, lately sending into France,
Did claim some certain dukedoms, in the right
Of your great predecessor, King Edward the Third.
In answer of which claim, the prince our master
Says that you savour too much of your youth,
And bids you be advis'd there's nought in France
That can be with a nimble galliard won;
You cannot revel into dukedoms there.
He therefore sends you, meeter for your spirit,
This tun of treasure; and, in lieu of this,
Desires you let the dukedoms that you claim
Hear no more of you …
KING HENRY: What treasure, uncle?
EXETER: Tennis-balls, my liege.
KING HENRY: … When we have match'd our rackets
to these Balls,
We will in France, by God's grace, play a set
Shall strike his father's crown into the hazard.

William Shakespeare, *Henry V*

The President is nothing more than a well-meaning baboon ... I went to the White House directly after tea where I found "the original Gorilla" about as intelligent as ever. What a specimen to be at the head of our affairs now!

General George McClellan on
President Abraham Lincoln

A savage old nabob with an immense fortune, a tawny complexion, a bad liver, and a worse heart.

Thomas Babington Macaulay of Lord Clive of India

Lord Sandwich: 'Pon my soul, Wilkes, I don't know whether you'll die upon the gallows or of the pox.
Wilkes: That depends, My Lord, whether I embrace your Lordship's principles, or your Lordship's mistresses.

Sir Charles Petrie, *The Four Georges*

The government has turned its back on the country and now has the impudence to claim the country is behind it.

F.E. Smith (1st Earl of Birkenhead) of the Liberal Government

A sheep in sheep's clothing.

Sir Winston Churchill of Clement Attlee

The people are tired of a man who has not an idea above a horse or a cigar ...

Joseph Brown on Ulysses S. Grant

An improbable creature, like a human giraffe, sniffing down his nostril at mortals beneath his gaze.

Richard Wilson of de Gaulle

A joke on his lips is no laughing matter.

Richard Brinsley Sheridan of the Earl of Lauderdale

John Randolph : I never sidestep skunks
Henry Clay: I always do.

    After Henry Clay had stepped out of the way of his rival John Randolph: Robert V. Remini, *Henry Clay*

Let Sporus tremble – "What? That thing of silk,
Sporus, that mere white curd of ass's milk?
Satire or sense, alas! Can Sporus feel?
Who breaks a butterfly upon a wheel?"
> Of the English politician Lord Hervey: Alexander
> Pope, *An Epistle to Dr Arbuthnot*

I have never seen a human being who more perfectly
represented the modern conception of a robot.
> Sir Winston Churchill of Molotov

A sophistical rhetorician, inebrieted with the
exuberance of his own verbosity.
> Benjamin Disraeli of Gladstone in
> *The Times*, 29 July 1878

Blaine! Blaine! J.G. Blaine!
Continental Liar from the State of Maine.
Of the American politician James Gillespie Blaine:
campaign slogan, 1884 election

His inconstancy is his great constant.
Eric Dupin of François Mitterand:
New York Review of Books, 3 November 1994

Senator McCarthy, my gardener may call me Alice, all
New York taxi drivers may call me Alice, the
policeman and the trashman may call me Alice, but
you may call me Mrs. Longworth.
Alice Roosevelt Longworth to Senator Joe McCarthy
who called her by her first name: attrib.

I decided the worst thing you can call Paul Keating, quite frankly, is Paul Keating.

John Hewson on his Labour rival

Voice from the crowd at a political rally when Oswald Mosley raised his arm in a facist salute: "All right, Oswald, you may be excused!"

Anon

He played too much football without a helmet.

Lyndon B. Johnson of Gerald Ford

The foreign policy of the noble Earl [Russell] may be summed up in two short homely but expressive words: – "meddle and muddle."

Earl of Derby, Speech in the House of Lords, 1864

Talk about the pews and steeples
And that cash that goes therewith
But the souls of Christian peoples.
Chuck it Smith!

> Response to F.E. Smith who had declared that
> the disestablishment of the Welsh Church "had
> shocked the conscience of Christian Europe":
> G.K. Chesterton, *AntiChrist, or the Reunion of*
> *Christendom*

A loose cannon on a rolling deck. He is not well-suited to the small-scale plot.

> Barry Jones on Gough Whitlam

A slur upon the moral government of the world.

> John Quincy Adams on Thomas Jefferson

Not while I'm alive 'e ain't.

> Ernest Bevin when told Aneurin Bevan was
> "his own worst enemy": M. Foot, *Aneurin Bevan*

～✿～

He can't see a belt without hitting below it.

> Margot Asquith on Lloyd George in the *Listener*,
> 11 June 1953

～✿～

On January 28, 1809 Napoleon summoned Talleyrand (his Foreign Minister) to the Tuileries, where a special meeting of the Grand Council was taking place:

Having whipped himself into a fury, Napoleon began pacing backward and forward between the fireplace and the table against which Talleyrand was leaning. For an hour, a flood of abuse and invective poured from the imperial lips. There was not a crime of which Talleyrand was not accused, not a blunder of Bonaparte's for which he was not blamed … Through it all, Talleyrand did not move a single muscle or indicate by a change of expression that he was aware of being addressed. Napoleon, irritated beyond endurance by Talleyrand's impassivity, lost all control – taunting him with his lameness, his wife's stupidity, and her infidelity. Finally, at the point of apoplexy, he howled, 'Answer me! What are your schemes? What is it that you want? Do you dare to tell me? I could break you into a thousand pieces, and I have the power to do it! But I hold you in too much contempt to take the trouble. Then, reverting to the language of the camp, he informed the Prince de Benevent, Vice-Grand-Chancellor of the Empire, Grand Chamberlain of the Imperial Court, that he was "shit in a silk stocking." Everyone sat in stunned silence, not daring to intervene. But the emperor had now exhausted his repertory and stamped to the door where he fired a last warning at Talleyrand: "Remember this: if there is a revolution, you will be the first to be crushed by it!" Then he was gone. It was not until then that Talleyrand came to life, and only, after a grave bow to his embarrassed colleagues to limp to the door and out into the corridor. To one of the ministers who followed him, he said, "What a pity that so great a man should be so ill-bred."

J.F. Bernard, *Talleyrand*

How do they know?
> Dorothy Parker on hearing the news that Calvin
> Coolidge had died: attrib.

George the Third
Ought never to have occurred.
One can only wonder
At so grotesque a blunder.
> Edmund Clerihew Bentley, *More Biography*

Son, in politics you've got to learn that overnight chicken-shit can turn into chicken salad.
> Lyndon B. Johnson when asked why he had
> embraced Richard Nixon after a controversial
> tour of South America in 1958:
> Fawn Brodie, *Richard Nixon*

The worst political appointment since Caligula made his horse a senator.

Of Lord North: anon

An Ambassador is an honest man sent to lie abroad for the good of his country.

Henry Wotton: written in the album
of Christopher Fleckmore

DEMOSTHENES: The Athenians will kill thee, Phocion, should they go crazy.
PHOCION: But they will kill thee, should they come to their senses.

Plutarch, *Parallel Lives*

She has the eyes of Caligula, and the mouth of Marilyn Monroe.

> François Mitterand of Margaret Thatcher

A pithecanthropoid.

> President Theodore Roosevelt of the President of Columbia

Here lies a great and mighty king
Whose promise none relies on;
He never said a foolish thing
Nor ever did a wise one.

> John Wilmot, Earl of Rochester, proposed epitaph on King Charles II

This is very true: for my words are my own and my actions are my ministers.

> Charles II's reply to the Earl of Rochester:
> Thomas Hearne, *Remarks and Collections*

Australian MP asks question: What is over sixteen stone and still a lightweight?
Answer: David Lange, the Prime Minister of New Zealand.

> Anon

You've got to put her in the same category as Bloody Mary, Queen Elizabeth I, Queen Anne and Queen Victoria. However, she reminds me most of Queen Elizabeth I out of those four. Her handling of men is not dissimilar. I mean, if you had been a courtier of Queen Elizabeth I, you would never have known quite whether you were going to get the treatment of an admired friend, or a poke in the eye with an umbrella.

Lord Hailsham of Margaret Thatcher

A hotbed of cold feet.

Abba Eban of the British Foreign Office

... like being savaged by a dead sheep ...

Denis Healey on being criticised by Sir Geoffrey Howe, House of Commons, 14 June 1978

So brilliant, yet so corrupt, who like a rotten mackerel by moonlight, shines and stinks.

John Randolph of Henry Clay: attrib.

I didn't fire him (General MacArthur) because he was a dumb son of a bitch, although he was, but that's not against the law for generals. If it was, half to three quarters of them would be in jail.

Harry S. Truman: Merle Miller, *Plain Speaking*

… a corpulent gentleman of fifty … a libertine over head and ears in disgrace, a despiser of domestic ties, the companion of gamblers and demi-reps, a man who has just closed half a century without one single claim on the gratitude of his country or the respect of posterity.

Leigh Hunt of George IV in *The Examiner*

He has sat on the fence so long that the iron has entered his soul.

Lloyd George of Sir John Simon: attrib.

A pig, an ass, a dunghill, the spawn of an adder, a basilisk, a lying buffoon, a mad fool with a frothy mouth ... and a lubberly ass ... a frantic madman.

Martin Luther of Henry VIII

He stands for what he thinks people will fall for.

Of a politician: anon

His coarseness of language and anecdote absolutely beggared description. His changes of mood between the aggressively ferocious and comradely genial never ceased to astonish me. He was a rhinoceros of a man with veins standing out on his forehead.

Lord Hailsham of Nikita Khrushchev

President Nixon's motto was, if two wrongs don't make a right, try three.

Norman Cousins, *Daily Telegraph*

I met Murder on the way –
He had a mask like Castlereagh –
Very smooth he looked, yet grim;
Seven blood hounds followed him:
All were fat; and well they might
Be in admirable plight,
For one by one, and two by two,
He tossed them human hearts to chew
Which from his wide cloak he drew.
  Of the British Prime Minister, Viscount Castlereagh:
      Percy Bysshe Shelley, *The Mask of Anarchy*

He has about as much backbone as a chocolate éclair.
      President Theodore Roosevelt of his
      predecessor President William McKinley:
      H.T. Peck, *Twenty Years of the Republic*

I compare it to something kept behind a curtain, about which there is a great deal of bustle and fuss, and a wonderful air of seeming solemnity; but when, by any accident, the curtain happens to be open, and the company see what it is, they burst into laughter.

Of the monarchy: Thomas Paine, *The Rights of Man*

Politicians are the same all over. They promise to build a bridge even where there is no river.

Nikita Khrushchev

A good politician is quite as unthinkable as an honest burglar.

H.L. Mencken, *Prejudices 4th Series*

Politics!? You couldn't get into politics! You couldn't get in anywhere. You couldn't even get into the men's room at the Astor.

Jean Harlow to Wallace Beery in *Dinner at Eight* (film)

No pig-eyed bag of wind is going to push us out of Berlin.

Frank Howley of Nikita Khrushchev

That youthful sparkle in his eyes is caused by his contact lenses, which he keeps highly polished.

Sheilah Graham on Ronald Reagan, *The Times*

O Gracious Queen we thee implore
To go away and sin no more.
Or if the effort be too great,
To go away at any rate.

Popular song at the time of the trial of
Queen Caroline, wife of George IV, in the
House of Lords, 1820

Like the silver plate on a coffin.

John Philpot Curran, Irish judge, describing Sir
Robert Peel's smile: Daniel O'Connell, *Hansard*,
26 February 1835

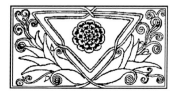

Mr Coolidge's genius for inactivity is developed to a very high point. It is far from being an indolent activity. It is a grim, determined, alert inactivity which keeps Mr Coolidge occupied constantly. Nobody has ever worked hard at inactivity, with such force of character, with such unremitting attention to detail, with such conscientious devotion to the task.

Of Calvin Coolidge:

Walter Lippmann, *Men of Destiny*

If he were a horse, nobody would buy him; with that eye, no one could answer for his temper.

Of Lord Brougham: Walter Bagehot,

Biographical Studies

… such a mongrel between pig and puppy, begotten by a wild boar on a bitch wolf, never before in any age of the world was suffered by the poltroonery of mankind to run through such a career of mischief.

John Adams of Thomas Paine: in Paul Johnson,
A History of the American People

Brilliant – to the top of his boots.

Lloyd George on Field Marshal Haig

I have seen better-looking faces on pirate flags.

Of Sir Alec Douglas-Home: anon

That grand imposter, that loathsome hypocrite, that detestable traitor, that ... opprobrium of mankind, that landscape of iniquity, that sink of sin, that compendium of baseness, who now calls himself our protector.

A Group of English Anabaptists referring to Oliver Cromwell in a letter to Charles II in exile

Yes I know Mr Davis. He is ambitious as Lucifer, cold as a snake, and what he touches will not prosper.

Sam Houston of Jefferson Davis

The Right Honourable Gentleman is reminiscent of a poker. The only difference is that a poker gives off occasional signs of warmth.

Benjamin Disraeli of Sir Robert Peel

A nonentity with side-whiskers.
>   Woodrow Wilson of Chester Alan Arthur:
>   attrib. in Marcus Cunliffe,
>   *American Presidents and the Presidency*

Get thee glass eyes; and, like a scurvy politician, seem to see the things thou dost not.
>   William Shakespeare, *King Lear*

He will be as great a curse to this country in peace as he was a squalid nuisance in time of war.
>   Sir Winston Churchill of Aneurin Bevan

Standing like a stork on the shores of Locarno.
>   Lloyd George on Austen Chamberlain

The dark, designing, sordid, ambitious, vain, proud, arrogant and vindictive knave.

> Charles Lee of George Washington

Pitt is to Addington
As London is to Paddington

> George Canning, *The Oracle*

A brutal vulgar man without delicacy or scholarship [who] looks as if he needed clean linen and should be put under a shower bath.

> Charles Sumner of Stephen Arnold Douglas:
> D.H. Donald, *Charles Sumner and the Coming of the Civil War*

A ravenous vulture who feeds on the dead and enfeebled … a swindling Maecenas, the Captain General of Iniquity … a heart dyed deep in blackness – gangrened to the very core.

> Edmund Burke, opening speech at the trial of
> Warren Hastings, 13 February 1788

Negotiating with him is like trying to pick up mercury with a fork.

> Lloyd George on Eamon de Valera
> (De Valera's response: "Why doesn't he use a spoon?"):
> M.J. MacManus, *Eamon de Valera*

As I sat opposite the Treasury Bench the ministers reminded me of one of those marine landscapes not very unusual on the coasts of South America. You behold a range of exhausted volcanoes.

> Benjamin Disraeli, Speech, Manchester,
> 3 April 1872

The manners of a cad and the tongue of a bargee.
Herbert Asquith of Joseph Chamberlain

A crafty and lecherous old hypocrite whose very statue seems to gloat on the wenches as they walk the States House yard.
William Cobbett of Benjamin Franklin

The hangman with his little bag came shuffling through the gloom.
American press comment on Viscount Runciman's mission to Prague in 1938

Mon Général, si vous m'obstructerez, je vous liquiderai.

Achieving of nothing – still promising wonders –
By dint of experience improving in blunders,
Oppressing true merit, exalting the base,
And selling his country to purchase his place.
A jobber of stocks by retailing false news
A prater at court in the style of the stews:
Of virtue and worth by profession a giber,
Of injuries and senates the bully and briber.
Though I name not the wretch, yet you know whom I
  mean –
'Tis the cur-dog of Britain, and spaniel of Spain.
Jonathan Swift of Sir Robert Walpole

It is a pity the cannibals do not get hold of this man.
Anonymous comment on Marcus Moziah Garvey:
Robert G. Weisbord, *Marcus Garvey, Pan-Negroist*

An alliance with him is like going for a walk with a grasshopper.
Lloyd George on Lord Northcliffe

Thomas Dewey is just about the nastiest little man I've ever known. He struts sitting down.
Mrs Clarence Dykstra: James T. Patterson,
Mr Republican, a biography of Robert A. Taft

The public be damned!
William Henry Vanderbilt, Reply to a question
whether the public should be consulted about luxury
trains: A.W. Cole, Letter, *New York Times*,
25 August 1918

The courtiers who surround him have forgotten
nothing and learnt nothing.
Marechal Dumouriez of Louis XVIII's court,
September 1795

A political leader worthy of assassination.
Irving Layton on Pierre Trudeau

In defeat unbeatable; in victory unbearable.
Sir Winston Churchill of Viscount Montgomery:
E. Marsh, *Ambrosia and the Small Beer*

That man has offered me unsolicited advice for six years, all of it bad.

> Calvin Coolidge of Herbert Hoover

⁓⁓⁓

… His fingers are as fat as grubs
And the words, final as lead weights, fall from his lips,

His cockroach whiskers leer
And his boot tops gleam.

… And every killing is a treat
For the broad-chested Ossete.

> Osip Mandelstam, *Epigram on Stalin*:
> in Nadezhda Mandelstam, *Hope Against Hope*
> (translated by Max Hayward)

⁓⁓⁓

He would make a drum out of the skin of his mother in order to sound his own praises.

> Lloyd George on Churchill

Retire, O Gideon, to an onion farm
Ply any trade that's innocent and slow
Do anything, where you can do no harm
Go anywhere you fancy – only go.

Of Gideon Welles: published in
Frank Leslie's Monthly, 1862

He is forever poised between a cliché and an indiscretion.

Harold Macmillan on Anthony Eden

Asked what he thought of the Reformed Parliament, when for the first time he surveyed the new Members of Parliament from the Peers' Gallery, the Duke replied: "I have never seen so many bad hats in my life."

Sir William Fraser, *Words on Wellington*

In Cabinet, he is worth his weight in brass — sounding brass.

Lloyd George on Curzon

There is no reason to attack the monkey when the organ-grinder is present.

Aneurin Bevan about Selwyn Lloyd ["the monkey"]
and Harold Macmillan: Speech, House of Commons,
16 May 1957

They couldn't pour piss out of a shoe if the instructions were written on the heel.

Lyndon B. Johnson of the
Association of American States

During his speech, [at the Security Council of the United Nations] Macmillan made a number of points with which Khrushchev disagreed strongly. In the end, Khrushchev became so enraged ... that he took off one of his shoes and banged the heel on the table in protest. Displaying his typically British style and aplomb, and not appearing in the least perturbed by Khrushchev's outrageous insult, Macmillan asked urbanely, "I wonder if I could have a translation?"

Greg Knight, *Honourable Insults*

... a guttersnipe is a gentleman compared to him.

Harry S. Truman on Paul Hume

The General has dedicated himself so many times, he must feel like the cornerstone of a public building.

Adlai Stevenson of Dwight Eisenhower: Jonathon Green (ed.), *Cassell Dictionary of Insulting Quotations*

They died with their drawn salaries in their hands.
  Lloyd George on the 1905 Conservative government

They they sit, like inverted Micawbers, waiting for
something to turn down.
        Of the Admiralty committee for examining
      inventions: Philip Guedalla, Speech at the Oxford
                                          Union, 1912

A Californian nut-case.
                  Press comment on Ronald Reagan

Earl of Chatham, William Pitt: If I cannot speak standing, I will speak sitting; and if I cannot speak sitting, I will speak lying.

Lord North: Which he will do in whatever position he speaks.

Jonathon Green (ed.),
Cassell Dictionary of Insulting Quotations

A number of anxious dwarfs trying to grill a whale.

Of politicians: J.B. Priestley, *Outcries and Asides*

Filthy Story-Teller, Despot, Liar, Thief, Braggart, Buffoon, Usurper, Monster, Ignoramus Abe, Old Scoundrel, Perjurer, Robber, Swindler, Tyrant, Field-Butcher, Land-Pirate.

Of Abraham Lincoln: *Harper's Weekly*

A piratical old bruiser with a first-class mind and very
bad manners.

> Lord Hailsham of Denis Healey

I thought he was a young man of promise; but it
appears he was a young man of promises.

> Arthur James Balfour of Winston Churchill:
> Randolph Churchill, *Winston Churchill*

did you ever
notice that when
a politician
does get an idea
he usually
gets it all wrong

> Don Marquis, *archys life of mehitabel*

I doubt even the Premier's ability to handle the petty-cash box at a hot-dog stand at the local Sunday School picnic.

George Moss of Sir Henry Bolte

All political parties die at last of swallowing their own lies.

John Arbuthnot: Richard Garnett, *Life of Emerson*

The daughter of debate, that eke discord doth sow.

Elizabeth I on Mary Queen of Scots:
George Puttenham (ed.), *The Art of English Poesie*

He looked as though he had been rough-hewn with an axe and needed smoothing down with a jackplane.

> Of Abraham Lincoln by his father:
> Paul Johnson, *A History of the American People*

~·❧·~

Rather than go through that again, I would prefer to have three or four teeth taken out.

> Hitler to Mussolini after having spent several hours
> in Franco's company: Paul Preston, *Franco*

~·❧·~

A becurled and perfumed grandee gazed at by the gallery gapers.

> James G. Blaine on Roscoe Conkling

He did not care in which direction the car was travelling, so long as he remained in the driver's seat.

> Lord Beaverbrook of Lloyd George,
> *New Statesman*, 1963

Must! Is must a word to be addressed to princes? Little man, little man! thy father, if he had been alive, durst not have used that word.

> Elizabeth I to Robert Cecil who had said that she
> must go to bed: J.R. Green,
> *A Short History of the English People*

Comrades, this man has a nice smile, but he's got iron teeth.

> Andrei Gromyko of Mikhail Gorbachev

A politician is a statesman who approaches every question with an open mouth.

Adlai Stevenson: attrib.

A lot of hard-faced men who look as if they had done very well out of the war.

Stanley Baldwin about the first House of Commons
elected after World War I:
J.M. Keynes, *Economic Consequences of the Peace*

Spare me the sight
Of this thankless breed,these politicians
Who cringe for favours from a screaming mob
And do not care what harm they do their friends
Providing they can please a crowd.

Euripides, *Hecuba*

Nixon is the kind of politician who could cut down a tree and then mount the stump and make a speech for conservation.

Adlai Stevenson: attrib.

The mere scum of the earth.

Duke of Wellington of his troops:
Philip Henry Stanhope,
Notes of Conversations with the Duke of Wellington

And thou a lunatic lean-witted fool,
Presuming on an ague's privilege,
Dar'st with thy frozen admonition
Make pale our cheek, chasing the royal blood
With fury from his native residence.

Richard II to his uncle John of Gaunt:
William Shakespeare, Richard II

He speaks to me as if I were a public meeting.

Queen Victoria of Gladstone:
G.W.E. Russell, *Collections and Recollections*

His mind is like an extinct sulphur-pit giving out the smell of rotten eggs.

Thomas Carlyle of Napoleon III

a politician is an arse upon
which everyone has sat except a man

e e cummings , 1 x 1, no 10

The forest laments so that the Prime-Minister may perspire.

> Lord Randolph Churchill on Gladstone's wood-cutting: in Lord Rosebery, *Memoirs*

Like being flogged with a warm lettuce.

> Paul Keating referring to an attack by the Opposition leader

If you start throwing hedgehogs under me, I shall throw a couple of porcupines under you.

> Nikita Khrushchev: *The Observer* "Sayings of the Week," 10 November 1963

Madam I may not call you; mistress I am ashamed to call you; and so I know not what to call you; but howsoever, I thank you.

> Elizabeth I (who disapproved of marriage among the clergy) to the wife of the Archbishop of Canterbury: John Harington, *A Brief View of the State of the Church of England*

... as silly a piece of Royalty as a man may meet.

> William Makepeace Thackeray of the Grand Duke of Weimar: quoted in Ann Monsarrat, *Willliam Makepeace Thackeray, An Uneasy Victorian*

AJAX: Thersites!

THERSITES: Agamemmnon, how if he had boils? Full, all over, generally?

AJAX: Thersites!

THERSITES: And those boils did run? Say so, did not the general run then? Were not that a blotchy core?

AJAX: Dog!

THERSITES: Then would come some matter from him: I see none now.

AJAX: Thou bitch-wolf's son, canst thou not hear? Feel then (*strikes him*)

THERSITES: The plague of Greece upon thee, thou mongrel beef-witted Lord!

William Shakespeare, *Troilus and Cressida*

A horrible voice, bad breath, and a vulgar manner – the characteristics of a popular politician.

Aristophanes

Chapter 6

PARTING SHOTS

Thou whoreson zed! Thou unnecessary letter!
William Shakespeare, *King Lear*

*Skakespeare sets the tone for a miscellany of insults to
store up for future use.*

It has been well said of Sigsbee H. Waddington that if men were dominoes he would be the double blank.

> P.G. Wodehouse, *The Small Bachelor*

Ettie has told enough white lies to ice a cake.

> Margot Asquith speaking of Lady Desborough:
> Nicholas Morley, *Julian Grenfell.*

A custom loathsome to the eye, hateful to the nose, harmful to the brain, dangerous to the lungs, and in the black stinking fume thereof, nearest ressembling the horrible Stygian smoke of the pit that is bottomless.

> James I (James VI of Scotland),
> *A Counterblast to Tobacco*

He is useless on top of the ground; he ought to be under it, inspiring the cabbages.

> Mark Twain

What he lacks in intelligence, he makes up for in stupidity.

Anon

Groucho Marx: I never forget a face, but in your case I'll be glad to make an exception.

Leo Rosten, *People I have Known, Loved and Admired*

Clare Boothe Luce: Age before beauty.
Dorothy Parker: Pearls before swine.

Attrib.

Don't point that beard at me, it might go off.

Groucho Marx

The unspeakable in pursuit of the uneatable.

Oscar Wilde on foxhunting: attrib.

"You are without exception the worst tick and bounder that ever got fatty degeneration of the heart through half a century of gorging food and swilling wine wrenched from the lips of a starving proletariat. You make me sick. You poison the air. Good-bye, Uncle Alaric," said Ricky drawing himself away rather ostentatiously. "I think we had better terminate this interview, or I may become brusque."

P.G. Wodehouse, *Uncle Fred in Springtime*

Judge to prisoner: Have you anything to say before I pass sentence.
Prisoner: Only this, your Honour, you are a nasty, chewed-up piece of string.

Anon

He's so nervous, he keeps coffee awake.

Anon

Alvanley – who's your fat friend?

> Beau Brummell of the Prince of Wales:
>> Capt. Jesse, *Life of George Brummell*

'Tis such fools as you
That makes the world full of ill-favour'd children.

> William Shakespeare, *As You Like It*

He is not only dull in himself, but the cause of dullness in others.

> Boswell, *Life of Johnson*

Queen Mary (Mary Tudor) to her council: My father made the better part of you out of almost nothing.

> A.L. Rowse

Judge Willis: Mr Smith, have you ever heard of a saying by Bacon – the great Bacon – that youth and discretion are ill-wed companions?

F.E. Smith: Indeed I have, your Honour; and has your Honour ever heard of a saying by Bacon – the great Bacon – that a much talking Judge is like an ill-tuned cymbal?

Judge (furiously): You are extremely offensive, young man.

Smith: As a matter of fact, we both are, and the only difference between us is that I am trying to be, and you can't help it.

The Life of F.E. Smith, First Lord Birkenhead,
by his son

The dawn of legibility gradually reveals his total inability to spell.

School report

I used to think it a pity that her mother, rather than she, had not thought of birth control.

Of Marie Stopes: Muriel Spark, *Curriculum Vitae*

Psychiatrist to patient: You haven't got an inferiority complex. You are inferior!

Cartoon caption in *The New Yorker*

He's so wet you can shoot snipe off him.

Anthony Powell, *A Question of Upbringing*

If I were the cream for that woman's coffee, I'd curdle.

Kathleen Howard in *Ball of Fire* (film)

Non amo te, Sabidi, nec possum dicere quare,
Hoc tantum possum dicere, non amo te!

Martial's epigram, paraphrased by the Oxford don Thomas Brown as:

I do not like thee, Dr Fell,
The reason why I cannot tell;
But this, I'm sure, I know full well,
I do not like thee, Dr Fell

The Right Hon. was a tubby little chap who looked as if he had been poured into his clothes and had forgotten to say "When!"

P.G. Wodehouse, *Very Good, Jeeves*

I said that I didn't think Chevy Chase could ad-lib a fart after a baked-bean dinner. I think he took umbrage at that a little bit.

Attributed to Johnny Carson

I regard you with an indifference closely bordering on aversion.

> Robert Louis Stevenson, *New Arabian Nights*

❧

I've met a lot of hard boiled eggs in my time, but you are twenty minutes.

> Billy Wilder, *Ace in the Hole* (film)

❧

Let the Dean and Canons lay their heads together and the thing will be done.

> Sydney Smith on a proposal to surround
> St. Paul's with a wooden pavement:
> H. Pearson, *The Smith of Smiths*

❧

Littlejohn, who in the farmyard of humanity would surely occupy a sty.

> Matthew Norman of a TV talkshow host: attrib.

O! he's as tedious
As a tired horse, a railing wife;
Worse than a smoky house. I had rather live
With cheese and garlic in a windmill, far,
Than feed on cates and have him talk to me
In any summer-house in Christendom.

Hotspur on Mortimer in William Shakespeare,
Henry IV, Part I

Remind me to have you stuffed.

Moe to Curly in *So Long Mr Chumps* (film)

She wore a low but futile decolletage.

Dorothy Parker

He's completely unspoiled by failure.

Noel Coward

Success turned his head. Too bad it didn't ring his neck a little.

Anon

~᛫~

You're like the toad, ugly and venomous.
William Shakespeare, *As You Like It*

~᛫~

Waldo is one of those people who would be enormously improved by death.
Saki (H.H. Munro), *The Feast of Nemesis*

~᛫~

A very weak-minded fellow I am afraid, and, like the feather pillow, bears the marks of the last person who has sat on him.
Earl Haig of Lord Derby: Letter to Lady Haig,
14 January 1918

You cannot hope
to bribe or twist,
Thank God! the
British journalist.
But, seeing what
the man will do
unbribed, there's
no occasion to.

Humbert Wolfe, *The Uncelestial City*

Judge: What do you suppose I am on the Bench for,
Mr Smith?
Smith: It is not for me, Your Honour, to attempt to
fathom the inscrutable workings of Providence.

The Life of F.E. Smith, First Lord Birkenhead,
by his son

Not a gentleman: dresses too well.

Bertrand Russell on Anthony Eden:
in Alastair Cooke, *Six Men*

Was it through his grandfather or his grandmother that he claimed his descent from a monkey?

Samuel Wilberforce to T.H. Huxley at a meeting of the British Association for the Advancement of Science, Oxford, June 1860: in *Macmillan's Magazine*, vol. 78

He had but one eye and the popular prejudice runs in favour of two.

Of Mr Squeers: Charles Dickens, *Nicholas Nickleby*

Judge: I have read your case, Mr Smith, and I am no wiser now that I was when I started.

F.E. Smith: Possibly, my Lord, but far better informed.

The Life of F.E. Smith, First Lord Birkenhead, by his son

The dogs bark but the caravan moves on.
>Company Chairman to shareholder who
questioned the chairman's increase in salary
at the Annual General Meeting: anon

Tonstant Weader Fwowed Up.
>Dorothy Parker, reviewing A.A. Milne's
The House at Pooh Corner in her Constant Reader
column in *The New Yorker*

The lunches of fifty-seven years had caused his chest
to slip down to the mezzanine floor.
>P.G. Wodehouse, *Chester Forgets Himself*

One cannot say she was dressed, she was clothed …
>Ivy Compton-Burnett of an old friend

Noel Coward was giving a series of wartime concerts for the Red Cross in Southern Rhodesia. He left Bulawayo: "after firing a brisk parting at an insistent lady reporter who kept asking whether he had anything to say to the *Star*. 'Yes,' replied Noel as his train drew out: 'Twinkle.'"

> Sheridan Morley, *A Talent to Amuse*

～⁂～

Dickie, you're so crooked that if you swallowed a nail you'd shit a corkscrew.

> Sir Gerald Templer to Lord Mountbatten:
> Philip Ziegler, *Mountbatten*

～⁂～

Ettie is so strong; she will be made into Bovril when she dies.

> Margot Asquith of Lady Desborough:
> Lord David Cecil, *The Observer Review*

– I changed my mind.

– Does it work any better?

Edward Arnold and Mae West
in I'm No Angel (film)

"If ever I meet that slimy, slinking, marcelle-waved by-product Pilbeam again," he said, "let him commend his soul to God! If he has time," he added.

P.G. Wodehouse, Summer Lightning

Would thou wert clean enough to spit upon.

Timon to Apemantus:
William Shakespeare, Timon of Athens

Everyone calls him "Webster." Words can't describe him.

Louis A. Safian

After his retirement Gill built himself a beautiful house in the country. The Vicar asked him why he never attended Church. This annoyed Gill, whose answer was, "For two very good reasons, Sir. The first is that, as Recorder of Chichester, I am prayed for in the Cathedral every Sunday morning; and the second, that I have defended more clergymen at the Old Bailey than any living barrister."

Cecil Whiteley, Brief Life

He's as phoney as a dentist's smile.

Louis A. Safian

TAILOR: She says your worship means to make a
    puppet of her.
PETRUCHIO: O monstrous arrogance. Thou liest,
 thou thread
Thou thimble,
Thou yard, three-quarters, half-yard, quarter, nail!
Thou flea, thou nit, thou winter-cricket thou!
Brav'd in mine own house with a skein of thread!
Away! Thou rag, thou quantity, thou remnant,
Or I shall so be-mete thee with thy yard
As thou shall think on prating whilst thou liv'st
I tell thee, I, that thou hast marr'd her gown.
        The tailor is scolded by Petruchio:
    William Shakespeare, *The Taming of the Shrew*

He is a fellow of a few, ill-chosen words.

                     Anon

The only infallible rule we know is that the man who
is always talking about being a gentleman never is one.
      Robert Smith Surtees, *Ask Mama*

There is a certain class of clergyman whose mendicity is only equalled by their mendacity.

> Archbishop Temple, Remark at a meeting of the
> Ecclesiastical Commissioners: quoted by
> Sir George Leveson Gower, *Years of Endeavour*

He looked at me as if I was a side dish he hadn't ordered.

> Ring Lardner, Jnr, referring to the American
> president W.H. Taft

The child remained there, drinking Cyril in for about half a minute; then he gave his verdict:

"Fish-face!"

"Eh? What?" said Cyril.

The child, who had evidently been taught at his mother's knee to speak the truth, made his meaning a trifle clearer.

"You've a face like a fish!"

> P.G. Wodehouse, *The Inimitable Jeeves*

She looks as bedraggled as a pigeon who got caught in a badminton game.

Anon

Martin, if dirt were trumps, what hands you would hold.

Charles Lamb:
Leigh Hunt, *Lord Byron and His Contemporaries*

… Impaling worms to torture fish.
On fishing: George Colman, *The Lady of the Wreck*

I've sometimes regretted living so close to Marie … because although I'm very fond of her, I'm not quite so fond of her company.

Marcel Proust, *Cities of the Plain, part II*

Achilles ... who wears his wit in his belly, and his guts in his head ...

William Shakespeare, *Troilus and Cressida*

~ ❧ ~

He is as artificial as manufactured ice.

Anon

~ ❧ ~

A man who could make so vile a pun would not scruple to pick a pocket.

Jon Dennis, *The Gentleman's Magazine*, 1781

~ ❧ ~

You dirty double-crossing rat!

James Cagney, *Blonde Crazy* (film)

~ ❧ ~

Client to hairdresser: Can you do a miracle?
Hairdresser: Darling, I am not a real fairy.

Anon

Sir, I have found you an argument; but I am not obliged to find you an understanding.

Dr Johnson: attrib.

She's the sort of woman … one would almost feel disposed to bury for nothing: and do it neatly, too!

Charles Dickens, *Martin Chuzzlewit*

Ye're a vera clever chiel, man, but ye wad be nane the waur o' a hanging.

The Scottish judge, Lord Braxfield, to a prisoner: Lockhart, *Life of Scott*

Gratiano speaks an infinite deal of nothing, more than any man in all Venice. His reasons are as two grains of wheat hid in two bushels of chaff: you shall seek all day ere you find them, and, when you have them, they are not worth the search.

William Shakespeare, *The Merchant of Venice*

Probably passed on, these many years, of an over dose of garlic, the way all New York barbers eventually go.

J.D. Salinger, *Seymour, An Introduction*

~{●}~

He has been educated beyond his intelligence.

Anon

~{●}~

The stork that brought you must have been a vulture.

Torrid Zone (film)

~{●}~

All God's children are not beautiful. Most of God's children are, in fact, barely presentable.

Fran Lebowitz

She's all right to look at but intellectually I don't reckon she can tell her fishcakes from her falsies.

Alan Ayckbourn, *Sisterly Feelings*

Espèce de bashibazouk!

Captain Haddock's favourite insult: Hergé, *Tintin*

Sir, you have but two topics, yourself and me. I am sick of both.

Boswell, *Life of Johnson*

I hear her hair has turned quite gold from grief.

Oscar Wilde, *The Importance of Being Earnest*